It's the Methodology, ✔ KU-699-052

Discover the complete ASIC Design flow including Behavioral Synthesis, Design Verification, Logic Synthesis, Test Synthesis, Static Timing Analysis, Parasitic Extraction and Floorplanning.

Trademark Information

UNIX is a registered trademark of UNIX System Laboratories, Inc.

Cadence is a registered trademark of Cadence Design Systems, Inc.

Verilog, Cell3, LEF, DEF, Silicon Ensemble, Pearl are registered trademarks of Cadence Design Systems, Inc.

Synopsys is a registered trademark of Synopsys, Inc.

Design Analyzer, Design Compiler, PrimeTime, Formality, Test Compiler, VHDL Compiler, HDL Compiler, Library Compiler, Simulation Graphical Environment (SGE), VHDL System Simulator, characterize, set_dont_touch, set_dont_use and set_dont_touch_network, Synthetic libraries, DC Expert, DC Professional, DesignTime, DesignWare, Floorplan Manager, are registered trademarks of Synopsys, Inc.

Mentor is a registered trademarks of Mentor Graphics Corporation.

BuildGates is a registered trademark of Ambit Design Systems, Inc.

Motive and ViewLogic is a registered trademark of ViewLogic Corporation.

VDSM is a registered trademark of Avant! Corp.

It's the Methodology, Stupid!

by

Pran Kurup

Taher Abbasi

Ricky Bedi

ByteK Designs, Inc.

World-wide Distributors:

ByteK Designs, Inc.

953 Industrial Avenue, Suite 108

Palo Alto, California 94303

email:bytek@bytekinc.com

Phone: (650)813-1230

http://www.bytekinc.com/

Library of Congress Cataloging-in-Publication Data

A C.I.P Catalogue record for this book is available from the Library of Congress.

Printed in the United States of America

To Lachmi, Shireen & Dipika

Table of Contents

Preface

The ever-increasing demand for integrated circuits, strict price/performance goals, time-to-market pressures and rapid developments in semiconductor process technologies are driving designs of 0.35 micron and below. These processes have come to be known as *deep sub-micron* (DSM) technologies or very deep sub-micron (VDSM), for no shortage of acronyms! With the rapid shrinking of process technologies, an entire range of issues including signal integrity problems such as on-chip cross talk, electromigration, off-chip simultaneous switching noise (SSN), ground bounce, power consumption and accurate parasitic extraction need to be addressed. This means that, as the industry moves to 0.35 micron and below, a new generation of design tools, methodologies and standards will be needed. The industry as a whole is taking steps to address this issue: Sematech is working with leading EDA vendors to develop a Chip Hierarchical Design System for Timing Driven Electrical and Physical Design. The Virtual Socket Interface (VSI) alliance is another effort aimed at driving standards that help achieve "systems on a chip". With the push for "system on a chip" and the development of the Virtual Socket Interface (VSI) standard to integrate IP from various sources on an ASIC, gate densities exceeding half a million gates are fast becoming common place. The VSI standard is an initiative by the major ASIC vendors,

EDA vendors, design houses and IP providers in the world to develop a standard specification to exchange embedded blocks developed by different sources.

With the advent of deep sub-micron technologies, conventional design flows and methodologies need to be appropriately enhanced. For example, emerging floor-planning tools are developed with front-end designers in mind. The intent is to provide designers greater control over the placement of design blocks, a better understanding of clock buffering and clocks skews, estimates of interconnect delays and wire-loads, early in the design flow. At the same time, verification of designs at different levels of abstraction is a serious challenge, largely due to increasing design sizes. Conventional gate-level simulation is fast becoming unrealistic for large designs. In the later part of the design flow, parasitic extraction and effective timing analysis techniques are critical.

ASIC design houses have, over the last decade, made a transition from proprietary in-house tools to commercial EDA vendor tools. This transition has brought with it a range of challenges for the design community. All EDA vendors have their core strengths and no EDA vendor provides all the tools (though they all claim to provide "complete solutions") required for the entire design flow. Instead, each vendor provides point tools which provide solutions in specific stages of the design flow. Further, EDA tools from different vendors don't always "talk to each other" (so much for standards!). This has resulted in the user community struggling to integrate these disparate tools. Most semiconductor houses use several point tools, resulting in an unwieldy concoction of in-house tools, commercially available tools and custom "just-in-time" kludges! CAD groups across the semiconductor industry are constantly challenged to develop methodologies that effectively utilize these point tools and incorporate new tools as they emerge.

As semiconductor and system companies battle the "spaghetti" of EDA tools and strive to establish a seamless design flow, clearly, Design Methodology has become a critical aspect of the design process. Very often, design teams are required to develop new methodologies, during the course of a project. As the title of this book indicates, we firmly believe that a pre-defined, well-documented Design Methodology, that accounts for all the strengths and limitations of existing commercial tools, is key to the success of any design project.

This book aims to provide the reader a design tool flow at the conceptual level avoiding reference to specific EDA tools as far as possible. It is meant to provide the ASIC designer a better understanding of the entire design flow—the concepts and methodologies involved at different stages in the flow, the traditional flows and its limitations and the back-end and its impact on the front-end of the design flow. The intent is to prepare the reader to make informed decisions about adopting and implementing new tools and methodologies with the overall flow in perspective. Some of the concepts and methodologies discussed in this book are already in use today, while others are new and emerging trends in ASIC design.

With incompatible tools, CAD engineers with their bag of tricks and engineering consultants (the panacea for all resource shortages or EDA tool ignorance!) have become an integral part of the ASIC design process. This book is also written with the CAD engineer and the engineering consultant in mind. It addresses issues, concepts and methodologies relating to behavioral synthesis, static timing analysis, design verification, test and logic synthesis, parasitic extraction and floor-planning. All examples are provided in both Verilog and VHDL. This book is not tailored to the structured custom designer. It also does not address issues such as design re-use, signal integrity and electromigration in detail.

Each chapter ends with a Methodology Audit. This section includes a list of top ten methodology queries that all design and CAD engineering teams must strive to address in order to meet the ASIC design challenges.

Our first book, Logic Synthesis Using Synopsys was tailored specifically towards synthesis using Synopsys tools. The rapid growth of the EDA tools, the challenges imposed by deep sub-micron designs and the dire need for seamless integration of disparate EDA tools, have together been the motivation for this book. This book is an amalgamation of the authors' combined experience across the design flow, ranging from front-end to back-end tools, training, tool development and usage, ASIC design, engineering management and consulting. Any feedback on this book can be sent to *bytek@bytekinc.com*.

Overview of Chapters

Chapter 1 begins with a description of the conventional ASIC design flow that is applicable to designs of 0.35 micron process technology and above. However, with shrinking process geometries, designers and EDA tools are faced with a whole slew of issues including parasitic effects, signal integrity issues, effective timing analysis, power estimation, floor-planning strategies etc. Hence, the design flow applied to present day ASICs is incapable of meeting the requirements of deep sub-micron designs. This chapter discusses the challenges imposed by deep sub-micron design and then presents an ASIC design flow tailored to its needs using state-of-the-art design methodologies.

The first step in the ASIC design flow after the specification of the design, involves high-level design capture. Several front-end design entry tools that generate structural VHDL/Verilog code from block diagrams and finite state machine tools that generate RTL code from bubble diagrams, are available. Alternately, designers capture design behavior in VHDL/Verilog at the register transfer level (RTL). However, the increasing complexity of present-day ASICs has resulted in the need for design description at the algorithmic level or at a higher level of abstraction. In other words, several designs require true behavioral description and behavioral synthesis as opposed to RTL description for logic synthesis.

Chapter 2 is devoted to Behavioral Synthesis concepts, features and methodologies. With logic synthesis in perspective, behavioral synthesis is introduced along with several key concepts such as chaining, multi-cycling and memory inferencing. One of the crucial aspects of behavioral synthesis is HDL coding at the algorithmic level as opposed to the RTL for logic synthesis. This requires testbenches that can deal with functional descriptions at the algorithmic level. This chapter also provides examples of HDL descriptions for behavioral synthesis and comparisons with RTL descriptions.

Chapter 3 covers design verification techniques. This chapter discusses HDL simulation in general, various types of simulators and their applications, and the limitations of conventional simulation methodology. Finally, emerging design verification methodologies such as cycle based simulation and formal verification are described and a strategy for migrating to these methodologies is proposed.

Chapter 4 discusses Logic Synthesis techniques such as applying constraints, compile strategies, resource sharing and allocation, clock specification for synthesis, critical path re-synthesis and optimization strategies. A simple case study is described to illustrate the concepts and strategies that can be applied to a given design.

With logic synthesis having become a critical component of the design flow, static timing analysis (STA) tools, which are often integrated with synthesis tools, have gained wider acceptance. Besides, with increase in size of ASICs, static timing analysis has become a viable alternative to compute-intensive gate-level simulations.

Chapter 5 covers static timing analysis. The usage and limitations of STA at different stages in the design flow—post-synthesis with statistical wire-load models, post-floorplan with estimated wire-loads and post place and route with RC-extracted parasitics, are discussed in detail. A simple example is used to illustrate the different static timing analysis concepts. A summary of commands is provided for three commercial STA tools namely, PrimeTime, Pearl and Motive.

Chapter 6 describes Test Methodology, including Test Synthesis and test concepts, in general. With the increasing demand for testability using partial scan or full-scan, test synthesis tools have become critical to the design flow. In this chapter, we discuss some basic test techniques and guidelines to be followed early in the design cycle. This chapter also discusses test synthesis techniques such as full scan, partial scan, scan styles, JTAG synthesis, ATPG and recommended design practices.

Chapter 7 is devoted to floor-planning and parasitic extraction. This chapter begins with an introduction to floor-planning and placement. Several do's and don't that need to be considered during these stages are provided. This is followed by a discussion on several file formats that enable the floor-planning process. Also discussed in this chapter are parasitic extraction and clock tree synthesis.

Acknowledgments

Several people contributed to the successful completion of this book. Sandya Krishna helped with the figures and in organizing the content. Theresa Gutierrez assisted in the printing, publishing and marketing efforts. Fred Gregarus of Fenwick & West LLP and his assistant Julie Yang, educated us on the legal aspects of the publishing business. Thanks also to Ercan Cetin, Shekhar Patkar, Hannes Froehlich, Adnan Sazli, Anand Surelia and Vasudevan Thyagarajan of ByteK Designs, Inc. for their support during various stages of this project. The Design Methodology team at Cirrus Logic deserves special mention for assisting and educating one of the authors through several designs from concept to silicon.

We thank our reviewers John Fernandes of Meropa, Inc., Prasad Saggurti of National Semiconductor and Amir Mottaez of Synopsys, Inc. for their invaluable feedback. We are specially grateful to J.Anandkumar of Cadence Design Systems for his unstinted support and useful tips and insights that helped shape the contents of this book. Without his help, this book would not be what it is today.

Of course, none of this would have been possible without the support and patience of our spouses—Lachmi, Shireen and Dipika—throughout this effort. Special thanks are due to Lachmi who designed the cover of this book and assisted with the formatting.

Pran Kurup
Taher Abbasi
Ricky Bedi

About the Authors

Pran Kurup is co-founder of ByteK Designs, Inc. Prior to this he served as Manager of Design Methodology at Cirrus Logic, Inc. in the corporate R&D department. At Cirrus, Pran was involved in ASIC design, development of design methodologies and in the evaluation of CAD tools. He received Corporate R&D awards for the successful development and deployment of In-place Optimization synthesis methodology and external IP Integration methodology. Prior to joining Cirrus Logic he was an Applications Engineer at Synopsys Inc. where he worked with several Synopsys customers supporting Synopsys tools, particularly the Design Compiler and interfaces to other EDA vendor tools. Pran is a co-instructor of the synthesis classes offered at the University of California, Santa Cruz Extension. He completed his undergraduate in Electrical Engineering from the Indian Institute of Technology, Kharagpur, in India and his Masters in Computer Engineering from the University of Miami, Coral Gables, in Florida. He has contributed articles for the ISD magazine, EDN-Asia magazine, the Synopsys Methodology Notes and application notes at Cirrus Logic, Inc.

Taher Abbasi is co-founder and President of ByteK Designs Inc., a design solutions company based in Palo Alto, California specializing in ASIC design, methodology development, training and contracting services. Prior to this, he was a Senior Design Applications Engineer at Synopsys, Inc. in Mountain View, California. He has worked with several Synopsys customers supporting the entire range of Synopsys tools, with special emphasis on the Test Compiler, the Behavioral Compiler, and the Design Compiler. His current interests include Behavioral Synthesis, Formal Verification and the development of methodologies using high-level design tools. He has been on consulting assignments at several leading system, EDA and semiconductor companies. Taher is a co-instructor of the synthesis classes offered at the University of California, Santa Cruz Extension, University of California, Irvine and California State University, Northridge. He completed his Masters in Computer Engineering from California State University, Northridge, and his undergraduate in Electronics Engineering from Bombay University, India.

Ricky Bedi, co-founder and Vice-President of ByteK Designs Inc., has over ten years of work experience in the EDA and semiconductor industry. He started his career at Viewlogic, where he worked in a broad range of areas including software and methodology development, ASIC design kits, training and consulting. He was instrumental in the design and development of a tool independent Library Database that enables programmatic generation of ASIC Libraries. He has worked with several design groups assisting in simulation, static timing analysis and developing effective tool flows. Prior to founding ByteK Designs, Inc., he was a Staff Engineer at Level One Communications Inc. in Sacramento, California. At Level One, he established comprehensive logic synthesis guidelines for HDL coding, design constraints and compile strategies. Further, he successfully integrated the synthesis methodology with datapath, static timing and clock tree synthesis tools. He received an outstanding achievement award for his contribution to Design Methodology at Level One. His current interests include Cycle based simulation and Formal Verification.

CHAPTER 1   *Show Me The Flow!*

Schematic capture based ASIC design that was pioneered in the early eighties, has since been replaced by RTL design capture and logic synthesis. However, rapid developments in fabrication technologies and the shrinking of semiconductor geometries, have ushered in an era of deep sub-micron technologies. As a result of this, the ASIC design flow has had to adapt to an entire range of new EDA tools and methodologies. Moreover, several of these tools are mostly point tools. In other words, these tools address specific needs of the flow and require other tools to complement them. Thus, irrespective of the set of tools used, unless they seamlessly blend into a comprehensive design flow, there is bound to be a need for kludges, hand-edits and scores of similar such quick fixes and not to mention eleventh hour heroics, all of which are error-prone. This means that there exists a dire need for a proven (or tested!), well documented and comprehended design flow, prior to the start of any design project.

This chapter is broadly divided into three sections. First, we briefly introduce the logic synthesis based design flow that is currently being followed for designs larger than 0.35 micron technologies. Then, we discuss the various design methodology challenges involved in the overall flow as designs increase in size and complexity. At each stage, different point flows are discussed. Finally, critical emerging technologies that have tremendous potential to significantly impact the design flow are introduced. All the methodologies introduced in this chapter are discussed in greater detail in subsequent chapters.

1.1 The Conventional ASIC Design Flow

As designs get larger and process geometries smaller, there are several design methodology challenges that arise. In order to better appreciate these challenges it is important to first understand the design flow (shown in Figure 1.1) for designs larger than 0.35 micron (the conventional design flow). This design flow begins with RTL design capture. The RTL design is then verified using logic simulation techniques. This is followed by logic synthesis (using statistical wire-load models) and test synthesis. Then, gate-level simulation is performed, followed by floor-planning and placement and routing. As a final iteration, loads after placement and route are back-annotated into the synthesis environment to perform in-place optimization.

The design flow described in Figure 1.1 has proven to be successful on several designs upto 0.35 micron process technologies. However, there are several issues that arise with the increase in complexity and speeds of designs, particularly, for designs under 0.35 micron technology. New tools and methodologies are required to be incorporated appropriately to enhance the flow shown in Figure 1.1. For example, design capture for high speed DSP applications could move to a higher level of abstraction i.e., from the RTL level to Behavioral (algorithmic) description. This in turn, requires the use of behavioral synthesis tools. Another, potential change is the transition from gate-level timing simulation to a combination of static timing analysis, cycle-based simulation and formal verification. As designs get larger, estimation of loading on interconnects early in the design cycle is critical. Thus, floor-planning at the front-end of the design flow namely, RTL floor-planning is gaining acceptance. Area-based placement and route has its limitations and is fast being replaced by a timing-driven approach.

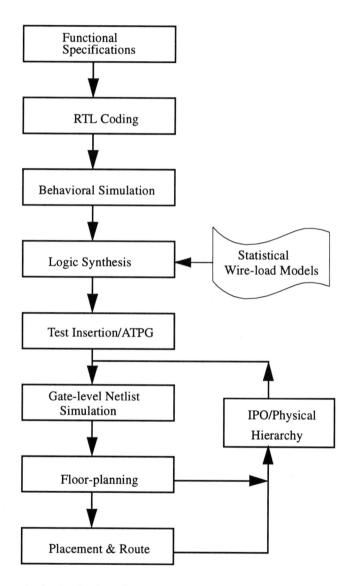

Source: Logic Synthesis Using Synopsys, Kluwer Academic Publishers

Figure 1.1 Logic Synthesis Based ASIC Design Flow

1.2 Design Methodology Challenges

In this section, we identify and describe the methodology challenges involved as ASIC designs transition to larger and more complex designs at deep sub-micron technologies. In particular, this section discusses methodology challenges involving wire-load models, design verification, floor-planning/placement and route, power and parasitic extraction. At each juncture, the point flows for the new methodologies are described.

As designs get larger and more complex, it is also required that several additional issues be addressed, some of which are from the realm of pc-board design. Signal Integrity (SI), for example, involves ensuring the signals in a design travel from their source to a destination without significant degradation. Noise due to interference with neighboring signals or cross-talk, reflections from impedance discontinuity, ground bounce due to poor power distribution are some of the causes for signal degradation. Analysis tools for signal integrity require that accurate library models be provided for the I/Os in the design. An increasing number of these models are provided in a common format called I/O-buffer information specification (IBIS).

Electromigration or metal migration involves the continuous bombardment of electrons on metal lines, which could cause shorts or interconnect failures. Another issue that requires attention as designs get larger and more complex is Electrostatic discharge (ESD). I/O ports are required to meet stringent ESD requirements. ESD occurs when two dissimilar materials come in contact and transfer charge producing a voltage between them. Protection against ESD can be internal to the IC or on the actual board. This book does not address ESD, signal integrity and electromigration issues.

1.2.1 Wire-load Models

With shrinking semiconductor geometries, delays due to the switching of transistors decreases. At the same time, delays due to physical characteristics such as resistance and capacitance of wires constitute a larger component of the overall delay. The logic synthesis design flow shown in Figure 1.1 involves the use of statistical wire-load models.

This means that, the wire load models available in the technology library are a statistical average based on several previous designs. Thus, the newer the technology, the smaller the number of designs that might have been targeted to it. Hence, the lesser the number of sample designs available to attain a representative statistical average.

The wire length in these wire load models is a function of the fanout. These are however, far from accurate given that fanouts and hence wire-load models are largely design specific. Moreover, statistical wire-load models assume an aspect ratio of 1 (i.e., all logic blocks are assumed to be square shaped). In reality, this need not necessarily be the case with designs, once they are placed and routed. In short, statistical wire-load models are far from accurate and it is imperative that there be a mechanism in the design flow for incorporating wire-loads which more accurately depict the physical topology of the distribution of cells in a given design.

Another significant challenge lies in achieving timing convergence between pre-layout and post-layout. The inaccuracy in the statistical wire-load models often results in the design not meeting timing requirements after layout. In other words, a design synthesized with statistical wire-load models and verified to meet timing requirements prior to placement and route is unlikely to meet the same timing requirements after placement and route. This means that the design has to be re-synthesized to meet timing constraints. A re-synthesis of the design implies a new placement and route iteration since re-synthesis causes changes in the netlist (both instances and net names). Thus, statistical wire-load models could result in several iterations between logic synthesis and placement and route before timing requirements are met.

The problem of timing convergence can be addressed by performing initial placement and generating estimated loads, which can be used to generate wire-load models specific to the design (also known as custom wire load model). Parasitic estimation is not based on actual routing data (as in the case of parasitic extraction) but estimated based on placement data. Custom wire-load models can be generated from within the floor-planning environment as shown in Figure 1.2 or from the synthesis environment after back-annotating the estimated loads generated from floor-planning. These custom wire load models can then be used to synthesize the design from RTL. Custom wire-load models are far more accurate because they are design specific and hence represent the physical topology of the current design rather than a statistical average of several designs. Thus, custom wire-load models are certain to improve the quality of the synthesis results.

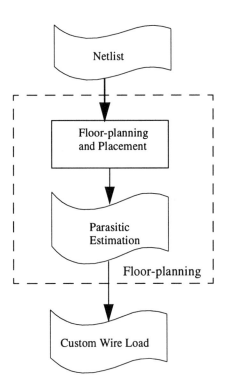

Figure 1.2 Custom Wire-Load Model Generation

1.2.2   Design Verification

There are two fundamental aspects to verification of a design, namely, functional verification and timing analysis. With increasing design sizes, conventional gate-level simulation (used for both functional as well as timing verification) is fast becoming too time consuming, compute intensive and limited in its ability to be an exhaustive verification strategy. Besides, gate-level simulation is limited by the number of vectors provided. As designs become faster and more complex, the challenge lies in being able to speed up the process of simulation-based timing analysis. Techniques like cycle-based simulation are beginning to be adopted to address this challenge. Chapter 3 discusses this technique in greater detail.

Static Timing Analysis (STA) is a faster (when compared to gate-level timing simulation), more exhaustive approach that does not require the generation of test vectors to determine the timing characteristics of a design. However, static timing analysis tools do not consider the functionality of a design. In other words, these tools are capable of identifying timing problems in the design but not functional problems. Static Timing analysis tools use delay information provided by delay calculators (which in turn are fed by estimated/extracted parasitics), and exhaustively calculates the timing slack across every path in the design.

STA tools are often integrated with synthesis tools since the optimization process is based on timing constraints. During the synthesis process, the actual delays computed by the STA tool built into the synthesis tool, are compared to the user specified timing constraints. For example, the static timing analysis tool called DesignTime from Synopsys is fully integrated into the Synopsys Design Compiler logic synthesis tool. Further, stand-alone commercial static timing tools are also available.

Appendix A lists a few commercial static timing analysis tools. Rather than completely replace logic simulation, static timing analysis is used today as an additional step in the design flow. It serves as a relatively quick check on the timing performance of the design.

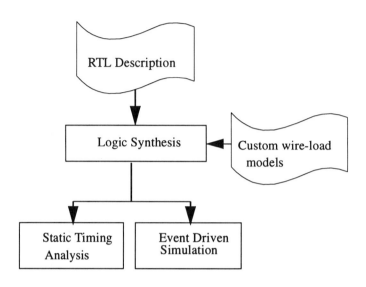

Figure 1.3 Pre-Layout/Post-placement Timing Analysis

Figure 1.3 shows the timing analysis flow using custom wire-load models. These custom wire-load models are based on parasitic estimation as discussed in section 1.2.1. The conventional STA flow involves the use of statistical wire-load models as in the case of the logic synthesis. However, it is imperative that both logic synthesis and pre-layout STA use custom wire-load models generated from placement data in order to ensure that post-layout and pre-layout timing converge with minimal iterations between the front-end (logic synthesis) and the back-end (place and route).

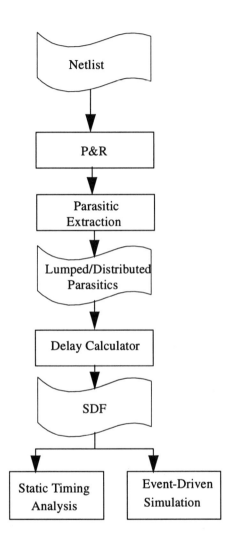

Figure 1.4 Post-layout Timing Analysis

Figures 1.4. shows the post-layout timing analysis flow which uses actual delay information based on parasitic extraction unlike the pre-layout/post-placement timing analysis flow which uses estimated parasitics. The static timing analysis tool usually takes in an SDF file generated using a Delay calculator or lumped/distributed parasitic information generated from parasitic extraction tools.

Thus, static timing analysis and gate-level simulation are two commonly used verification techniques. Pre-layout STA for designs smaller than 0.35 micron process technologies must use custom wire-load models, unlike statistical wire-load models used in conventional design flows. STA however, also has a number of challenges, such as identifying false paths and multi-cycle paths, breaking timing loops in the design etc. Chapter 5 discusses STA is greater detail. Emerging verification techniques such as Formal Verification and cycle-based simulation are discussed in greater detail in chapter 3.

1.2.3   Floor-planning, Placement and Routing

Logic synthesis and all the steps in the design flow prior to it are often referred to as the front-end. Similarly, floor-planning and placement and routing are referred to as the back-end. Unfortunately, the back-end is often treated as an "across the wall" activity. This approach is no longer feasible, especially with the advent of DSM designs. In other words, with the move to smaller process geometries and larger gate-count designs, the front-end and back-end should be tightly linked—the need for hierarchical placement and routing, the inaccuracy of statistical wire-load models, RTL floor-planning etc. being some of the reasons for tighter integration.

There are several challenges involving floor-planning and placement and route. Firstly, the need to achieve timing convergence between pre-layout and post-layout with minimal number of iterations between the front-end and back-end tools. A successful iteration between front-end and back-end tools is achieved when the design meets timing requirements after back-annotating parasitics generated from parasitic extraction after routing. In general, routing is an extremely compute intensive task. Hence, lesser the number of iterations between the front-end and the back-end, faster the overall duration of the entire design flow.

In deep sub-micron designs floor-planning/placement and route are extremely critical and can have a significant impact on the results. As processes shrink, overall delays in the circuit are increasingly dominated by interconnect. Below 0.35 micron the interconnect delay is often 50% of the total delay unlike close to 20% for larger technologies. This increasing proportion of interconnect delay, along with the large amount of interconnect on large ASIC designs, means that the existing statistical methods of calculating interconnect delay are no longer sufficiently accurate. Thus, preliminary floor-planning and estimation of parasitics need to be performed up-front, prior to actual routing, in order to minimize the potential vicious circle between front-end and place and route tools. The number of iterations can be significantly reduced by a transition to a "floor-planning and placement centric" flow. Custom wire-load models generated after parasitic estimation based on placement data are an absolute must when dealing with process technologies lesser than 0.35 micron. Besides, effective placement holds the key to the overall back-end process. Using estimated parasitic information generated from placement data up-front in the synthesis process, effectively bridges the gap between front-end and back-end.

Another challenge in placement and route methodology lies in the transition to a timing driven placement and route approach. This implies taking timing constraints into consideration during routing. In other words, it is essential to be able to specify signal delay limits for different nets in the design, especially critical nets. The greater the timing constraints or more the number nets with timing constraints, the longer it takes for the router to complete its task. Moreover, it is possible that the router might not achieve its task, since some timing constraints might be impossible to meet. However, in order to meet the timing requirements of today's high-speed chips, it is critical to perform routing using timing constraints. In addition, the router must adhere to signal integrity, electromigration, power and other such specifications.

An effective placement and route methodology requires the exchange of placement and timing information between front-end and back-end tools through Physical Data Exchange format (PDEF) or Standard Delay Format (SDF) constraint files. The transfer of timing information through SDF files is the key to the timing driven placement and route approach. However, SDF constraint files are usually generated only when the netlist is "completely" stable. The early iterations of placement and routing are not usually based on SDF constraint files.

1.2.4 Power

The drive towards system on a chip (SoC) has accelerated the significance of a low power design methodology. There are several aspects that drive the need for low power designs. Firstly, portable applications require extended battery life and low power dissipation. Secondly, these applications require a high level of reliability.

With decreasing transistor sizes and the growing demand for low power chips, it is critical to have an estimate of the overall power consumption in a chip prior to tapeout. In a typical IC, the I/O pads and the clock network together account for anywhere from 40% to 80% of the total power consumption. The sequential and combinational gates and the on-chip memories account for the rest.

The power consumed by a design can be divided into three parts— switching power, short circuit power and leakage power. Of these the switching power or the power consumed in charging and discharging the output capacitance of a gate is a significant component of the overall power. The short circuit power or the power consumed internal to a gate when its inputs change value contributes close to 20% of the overall power. The leakage power which happens through the substrate of the transistor layout is relatively small and is often ignored during power computations.

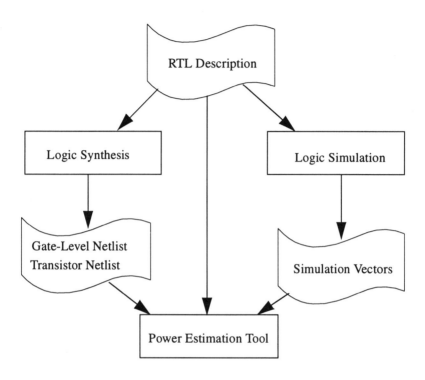

Figure 1.5 Power Estimation Flow

The challenges involved in design for low power include, power reduction at the RTL, power reduction at the gate level and most importantly, a low power design methodology. Firstly, power reduction can be achieved at the library level by the use of specially designed low power cells. Secondly, it is important that special design techniques be used in the RTL to ensure minimal power consumption. For example, clock gating can be used to reduce overall activity. Clock trees with minimal number of buffers is another technique that can be used to reduce power in clock networks. At the logic level, by deploying the required enabling logic, combinational logic in the design can be effectively "turned-off" when not in use, thereby reducing the power consumed. In short, while there are several techniques that can be used in order to reduce overall power in a design, the challenge lies in effectively incorporating these design practices along with several new tools and methodologies. Most importantly, it is critical that power issues be addressed early in the design process as opposed to late in the design flow.

There are two kinds of commercially available power tools—power estimation tools and power optimization tools. Power estimators as the name indicates, provide an estimate of the power consumed by a design based on switching activity. Appendix A lists a few commercially available power tools. Power optimization tools take into consideration power consumption of a design just as logic synthesis tools take into consideration timing and area. Power Compiler from Synopsys is an example of a tool capable of optimization for power. All power estimation tools require the use of vectors from simulation or I/O toggle probability rates and accurate tool libraries. Figure 1.5 shows the basic flow for power estimation.

1.2.5 Parasitic Extraction

As designs get larger, and process geometries smaller than 0.35 micron, the impact of wire resistance and capacitance on the overall delay becomes significant. Hence, techniques are required to accurately model both the resistance and the capacitance (also called parasitics) in a design. In the design flow, extraction of parasitics follows the layout and clock tree insertion steps. The output from parasitic extraction known as Detailed Standard Parasitic Format (DSPF) is fed to a delay calculator, which in turn drives the timing analysis process (both static timing and gate-level simulation) as shown in Figure 1.6. Hence, accurate extraction of parasitics is critical to delay calculation and hence to timing analysis. Appendix A lists a few of the several commercial parasitic extraction tools available.

Parasitic Extraction tools examine the structures in the physical design database and builds a netlist that models the parasitic capacitors and resistors in the design. Extraction tools have different techniques of modeling the resistance and capacitance (RC) in a circuit such as 3D, 2D, quasi-3D etc. Simple Layout Parasitic Extraction (LPE) tools examine the 2D structures in the physical database and calculate capacitance and resistance based on 2D geometries, and coupling capacitance based on simple 2D wire overlaps.

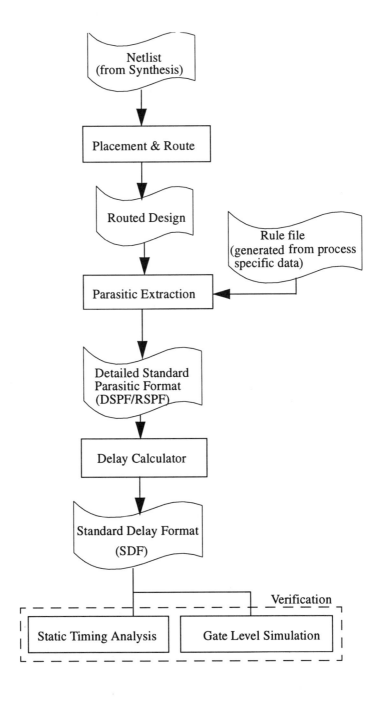

Figure 1.6 Parasitic Extraction Flow

Other tools more accurately model the 3D interfaces between physical structures, including capacitance due to inter-layer and intra-layer edge relationships.

One of the challenges with extraction is the run-time involved. Larger the design, greater the run time. Most commercial EDA vendor tools have several modes of extraction (level 1, level 3, level 7 and level 21 for the Arcadia tool from Synopsys, for instance) corresponding to different levels of accuracy. Greater the accuracy, longer the run time. To tackle the run time issues, EDA vendors have developed methodologies for distribution of extraction tasks across multiple machines.

Another issue with parasitic extraction is the large sizes of files generated. The RC network extracted from designs is often extremely large, running into the tens and hundreds of megabytes in size. In many cases, the number of capacitor and resistor elements in many of the nets can be reduced without significantly compromising accuracy. Most reduction tools give the user the ability to tune the reduction to trade off accuracy against netlist size.

1.3 Emerging ASIC Design Flow

This section describes the design methodology independent of specific EDA vendor tools and captures the flow at a conceptual level. Figure 1.7 shows the complete methodology flow from the behavioral description to the tapeout phase. We have used the term "emerging" primarily because some of the methodologies involved in this flow are still in the process of being widely adopted. This flow addresses the design methodology challenges discussed in section 1.2 without delving into the details involved in specific sub-flows. All references to specific EDA tools and file formats have been intentionally avoided in the figure.

The entire flow has been divided into four basic parts, namely, Design capture, Synthesis, Verification and the Back-end. These four parts of the design flow are very much interrelated and involve plenty of "back and forth" between these stages.

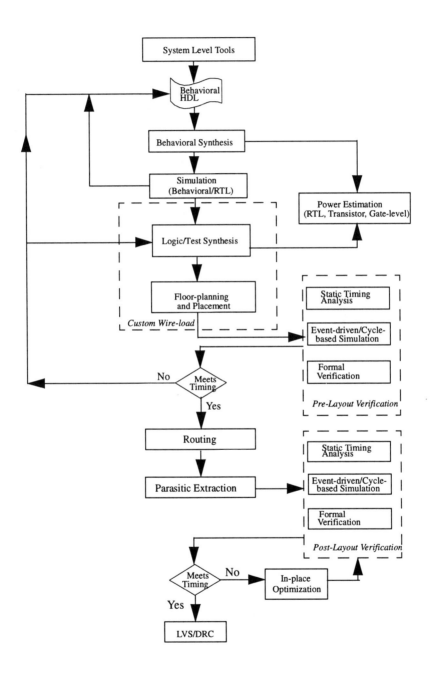

Figure 1.7 Design Methodology Flow

As designs move towards "system on a chip" it is often required to model the performance of a proposed system at a high-level prior to implementation. Commercially available tools such as BONeS from Cadence assist in performance modeling and analysis of throughput, latency, and resource sizing. Such tools help address fundamental issues such as—How effective can a system be? What are potential bottlenecks when you increase the bus width from 64 to 128? With increasing sizes of designs, it is critical to model its performance and identify potential bottlenecks prior to actual implementation of the design. For the purpose of the design flow shown in Figure 1.7, we assume a design specification exists and is to be implemented.

1.3.1   Design Capture

Design Capture can be divided into three possible categories: *Schematic capture, RTL description and Behavioral Description.* Schematic capture was the means of design entry, in particular, prior to the introduction of logic synthesis. Design capture then moved to the RTL level with the inception of logic synthesis tools like the Synopsys Design Compiler. However, with increasing size and complexity of designs and the need for "system on a chip" levels of integration, EDA tools that permit design capture at a higher level of abstraction, namely at the behavioral or the algorithmic level are critical. This implies a change in coding style from the RTL to an algorithmic approach. In RTL descriptions, the design is specified in terms of expressions, clocks and registers, manually binding operations to specific clock periods. Thus, RTL descriptions restrict the exploration of the design space. On the other hand, in behavioral descriptions functionality is described by which operations must occur, not by how they are implemented in hardware. Chapter 2 discusses behavioral synthesis in greater detail while Chapter 4 is dedicated to logic synthesis.

1.3.2   Synthesis

The entire process of synthesis can be divided into three parts, namely, *behavioral synthesis, logic synthesis and test synthesis.* Together these three parts determine the transition from "code" to a gate-level netlist. Design capture at the algorithmic level requires the use of behavioral synthesis tools. These tools assist the designer to make trade-offs and decide on an optimal architecture for a certain specification. Further, they are capable of arithmetic optimization, pipelining, automatic generation of the control FSM, and in general, help identify the best implementation that meets latency and area goals. In the design flow logic synthesis is preceded by behavioral synthesis. The output from behavioral synthesis is synthesizable RTL which in turn serves as the input to logic synthesis. Chapter 2 describes behavioral synthesis in detail.

For designs involving RTL design capture, logic synthesis is the practical next step. Logic synthesis tools infer gates from RTL to meet constraints such as timing, area and power. Another increasingly critical aspect of design is test or scan synthesis and test pattern generation. Scan insertion was until recently a post-synthesis activity. However, as designs get larger and timing critical, it is required that test synthesis be integrated into the logic synthesis phase. This helps address the timing delays and area overhead due to scan earlier in the design flow rather than after netlist generation. Thus, it is essential that there be a "one-pass synthesis" which combines both logic and test synthesis. Chapter 3 discusses logic and test synthesis, while chapter 6 discusses test methodology.

1.3.3   Design Verification

As the design traverses through different levels of abstraction such as RTL, gates, layout etc. it is crucial that the design be verified at each of these stages. In particular, deep sub-micron effects if not considered appropriately, could result in poor verification and hence faulty designs.

Verification can be divided into four basic techniques, namely, *Event-driven simulation, Cycle-based simulation, Formal Verification and Static Timing Analysis.* Of these, event-driven simulation is used extensively today. Most commercially available simulation tools belong to this category. Cycle-based simulation, formal verification and static timing analysis are collectively trying to address the limitations of event-driven simulation by dividing the verification task into: timing verification (static timing analysis at the gate-level or transistor level both pre and post-layout), functional verification (cycle-based simulation at the HDL level) and equivalence checking (formal verification between HDL and gates). Chapter 3 discusses event-driven and cycle-based simulation in detail and introduces formal verification. Static Timing Analysis is discussed in chapter 5.

1.3.4   The Back-End

Floor-planning, Placement & Routing, parasitic extraction and Layout versus schematic/Design Rule Checking (LVS/DRC) together constitute the "back-end" effort. However, with the need to use custom wire-load models, floor-planning early in the design cycle is critical. Thus, after logic synthesis and verification, floor-planning and placement are performed, followed by parasitic estimation. Custom wire-load models are generated using estimated parasitics and this in turn drives the synthesis process. However, it is important that the estimates generated from floor-planning are identical (or close) to those determined by the router during the routing process.

Figure 1.8 shows the high-level back-end flow beginning with logic synthesis. This flow assumes that custom wire-load models have been generated and that the netlist from logic synthesis is largely stable. Deep sub-micron designs require that placement and routing be timing-driven rather than area based. This means the cell libraries for placement and routing will additionally require timing information in them. In order to perform timing-driven placement and routing, it is required to generate path constraints for the design. These constraints are derived from the constraints provided to the logic synthesis tool. These constraints can be in the form an Standard Delay Format (SDF) constraint file. The SDF constraint file generated from logic synthesis is usually not used to drive the placement and routing tool until the netlist is stable.

Placement and routing for larger designs, in particular, is likely to be hierarchical. This means that individual blocks in the design are routed, extracted and analyzed separately (assuming that logical and physical hierarchies are the same), just as different blocks are synthesized in logic synthesis. At the top level, these blocks can then be routed to generate the complete layout database. However, several design houses still use the flat placement and route techniques.

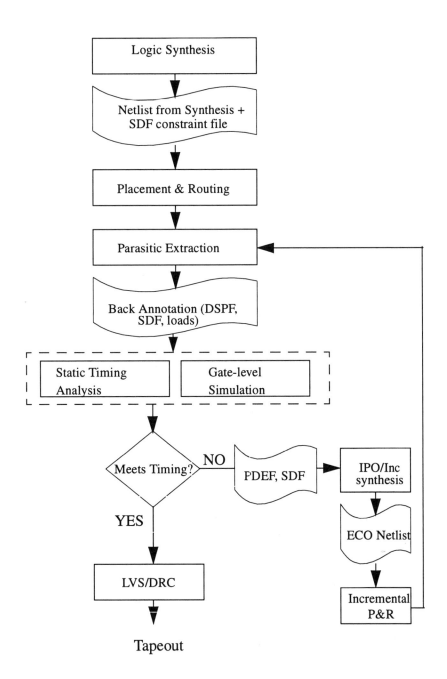

Figure 1.8 High-Level Post-Synthesis Flow

After placement and route, parasitic extraction is performed on the design. These parasitics are then used to verify the timing characteristics of the design. If the timing requirements are not met, the parasitics (along with placement information in the form of PDEF) are used to perform in-place optimization (IPO) within the logic synthesis environment. Alternately, place and route tools are also capable of performing IPO. The result of an IPO is an Engineering Change Order (ECO) netlist. During the IPO process the existing instance names and net names are retained. The only changes that occur in the netlist are due to addition of buffers and re-sizing of cells. Placement and Route tools are capable of using the existing routed database and incorporating the incremental changes introduced during the IPO process. The final steps in the design flow involve physical verification (LVS) and design rule checking.

1.4   Emerging Design Methodologies

Several new and exciting tools and methodologies that can significantly impact the design flow are constantly being developed and implemented. These methodologies are still in the process of gaining widespread usage, but have tremendous potential to enhance the overall flow. In this section, we consider a few of these technologies, namely, behavioral synthesis, formal verification and cycle-based simulation.

1.4.1   Behavioral Synthesis

Most current design flows involve description at the RTL level which is then synthesized using a logic synthesis tool. This however, limits architectural flexibility. In other words, to explore multiple architectures for a given specification, one has to re-write the RTL code. This exercise is time consuming and unrealistic. In addition, logic synthesis optimizes a design in two dimensions: to meet timing and area constraints (not counting synthesis tools for power). Further, logic synthesis optimizes combinational logic between registers, but not the registers themselves.

While designs increase in complexity, it is critical to capture designs at the algorithmic level or at a higher level of abstraction and explore different implementations of a design using the same HDL description. This requires the usage of Behavioral synthesis tools that can do the appropriate trade-offs and perform high-level operations such as chaining, multicycling and memory inferencing. Two basic concepts that are fundamental to behavioral synthesis are latency and throughput. Throughput is the minimum number of clock cycles between sets of data being fed to the inputs of a design. Latency on the other hand, is the

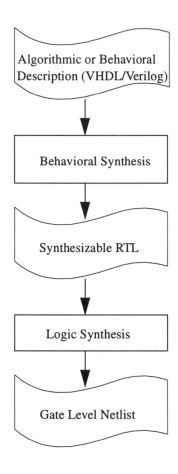

Figure 1.9 Behavioral Synthesis Flow

minimum number of cycles required to process a set of data. The objective of behavioral synthesis is to derive an optimal architecture that meets latency and clock period requirements from different functionally equivalent implementations.

Wire-load models provide a serious challenge to behavioral synthesis. Very often, synthesized netlists which appear to meet timing prior to placement and routing, fail to meet timing after back annotation of parasitic data. At smaller geometries this discrepancy is likely to be greater because of the larger wire delays. This problem is due to the use of statistical wire-load models during logic synthesis. These wire-load models are often inaccurate—either too optimistic or pessimistic and lack an understanding of placement information specific to the design. This affects both behavioral synthesis and logic synthesis tools. To address this issue, behavioral synthesis tools (like logic synthesis tools) must provide a means to generate custom wire-load models and use them for estimating interconnect delay up front.

Figure 1.9 shows the behavioral synthesis flow beginning with the source behavioral HDL. Behavioral synthesis requires that a particular coding style be followed. It is capable of assisting the user to explore alternate design architectures by changing constraints with minimal or no change to the source HDL. The behavioral synthesis tool makes architectural implementation decisions based on cycle-period, latency and throughput goals. The algorithm to start with, must be an efficient one, in order to guide the synthesis tool to an optimal implementation. Another constraint is that the design must be fully synchronous. Chapter 2 discusses behavioral synthesis in greater detail.

1.4.2   Formal Verification

As designs increase in size, and process technologies shrink, conventional verification techniques are fast spiraling out of control. For example, event-driven gate-level logic simulation for large designs require huge number of vectors and the associated run times are usually unacceptable.

Equivalence checking (the most common form of Formal Verification) is a mathematical approach to verify equivalence of a reference design and a revised design. Verification is done without the need for test vectors. Thus, it is faster than logic simulation. However, it performs only function equivalence checking and does not consider timing. Chapter 3 discusses formal verification in greater detail.

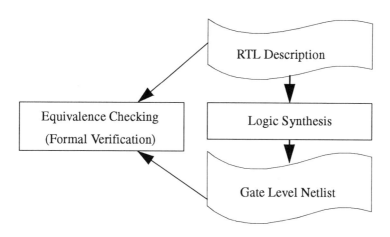

Figure 1.10 Formal Verification Flow

Appendix A lists a few of the commercially available formal equivalency checking tools. In general, equivalence checking tools can be applied to compare any two different levels of abstraction—RTL to gates, RTL to RTL, gate-level to gate-level, pre-layout netlist to post layout netlist as shown in Figure 1.10. Several commercial Formal Verification tools are currently available and its usage as a fundamental component of the design flow is gaining acceptance.

1.4.3   Cycle-Based Simulation

The increasing size of ASICs has resulted in the rapid increase in the number of vectors required to test the device and the simulation run times. To address this bottleneck, a combination of methodologies including static timing analysis, formal verification and cycle-based simulation is fast gaining acceptance. While static timing analysis checks for timing, formal verification checks to see that the design remains functionally identical when going through different levels of abstraction such as synthesis, RTL, test and layout.

Cycle-based simulation on the other hand checks for functionality of a design at the RTL and gate-level. It offers verification speeds of 100 to 1000 cycles per second on large designs. It is a technique whereby an entire synchronous design is partitioned into a series of storage elements and combinational logic. There are no delays in cycle simulation and every storage element is computed in every cycle, eliminating the need to schedule events and the need to evaluate signals between cycle boundaries. In contrast, event driven simulation requires that several functions be evaluated multiple times in a single clock cycle, causing it to be time consuming and complicated. However, cycle based simulation requires that the design be fully synchronous. This could mean partitioning the design if it is not fully synchronous and also re-writing test benches suited to cycle behavior. Chapter 3 discusses cycle-base simulation in greater detail.

1.5 Methodology Audit

1. Do you follow specific conventions such as standard procedures for naming signal, ports, modules, buses etc. during all stages of the design flow?

2. Do you have a completely documented and verified design flow prior to the start of the design project?

3. Is Static Timing Analysis part of your current verification flow?

4. Are you currently using a timing driven placement and route methodology?

5. Is power estimation (at the RTL, gate-level and transistor level) a part of your current design flow?

6. If you are working on designs at 0.35 micron and below, do you use signal integrity/cross-talk analysis tools?

7. Do you follow a hierarchical placement and route methodology? If so, does the extraction tool also support a hierarchical flow?

8. Do you distribute the task of parasitic extraction across multiple machines? This technique helps significantly improve the run-time.

9. Is your design targeted for high speed DSP applications? If so, have you considered the use of behavioral synthesis tools?

10. Do you have an estimate for the margin of error for the parasitic extraction tool? In other words, do you have any data for silicon correlation with delays calculated using back-annotation information after parasitic extraction?

CHAPTER 2

A Behavioral Synthesis Primer

What is behavioral synthesis? How is it different from conventional logic synthesis? What are the fundamental concepts of behavioral synthesis? What impact does behavioral synthesis have on the overall design flow and what are the challenges involved? The objective of this chapter is to address each of these issues and to familiarize and educate the reader about behavioral synthesis technology in general and its applicability to a design flow.

This chapter is organized as follows. First we introduce the concept of behavioral synthesis and the design flow using behavioral synthesis. Then, we describe the features of conventional behavioral synthesis tools. Simple conceptual examples have been provided at different stages of the discussion. Then, we discuss the challenges involved in making the transition to behavioral synthesis. Finally, a behavioral description of an Infinite Impulse Response Filter is described in both VHDL and Verilog to illustrate the concepts. The chapter ends with a methodology audit that is applicable to both current and future users of behavioral synthesis.

2.1 Behavioral Code Vs. RTL Code

Synthesis tools—logic and behavioral synthesis tools—support both VHDL and Verilog HDL, the two current industry standard hardware description languages. Further, both logic synthesis and behavioral synthesis tools support the same language constructs. However, the coding style required for behavioral synthesis is very different from that used for logic synthesis. The HDL written for logic synthesis is commonly referred to as RTL code. In this style of coding, clock cycle to clock cycle operations and events are explicitly defined. In other words, the architecture of the design is implicit in the RTL code. The logic synthesis tool automatically converts this RTL code into gates without modifying the implied architecture. Thus, during logic synthesis the architecture of the design is pre-defined and the synthesis tool tries to optimize the gate-level implementation of the design to meet timing and area goals. For example, an adder can be implemented in one of many ways—carry-look forward, carry look ahead, ripple adder etc.

Example 2.1   Illustration of Behavioral vs. RTL code

```
wait for clock rising edge
sum = A*B - C*D;
```

The same HDL can be read into both behavioral and logic synthesis tools but will produce different results. Consider the high-level description shown in Example 2.1 which involves five variables A, B, C, D and SUM. There are three operations defined namely, two multiplications and one subtraction "*" "*" and "-").

The above example is interpreted differently by both logic synthesis and behavioral synthesis. Since logic synthesis infers the architecture of the design from the HDL code, it tries to optimize the logic to perform all the three operations within one clock cycle unless explicitly specified as a multi-cycle path. Further, it aims to meet the desired clock period and area constraints. However, logic synthesis is incapable of moving these operations across different clock cycles based on timing information of operations, input arrival times etc. Behavioral synthesis helps address this limitation. Just as HDL written for logic synthesis is called RTL, HDL written for behavioral synthesis is called behavioral HDL.

Behavioral HDL describes the intent and the algorithm behind the design without specifying the cycle to cycle behavior. Thus, the same behavioral HDL can be used to produce different functionally equivalent architectures with independent timing characteristics. In addition, behavioral synthesis automatically generates the state machine for all architectures of the design. For instance, in Example 2.1, behavioral synthesis could identify a particular architecture that can perform all the operations in one clock cycle at the desired clock period. Alternately, the tool could identify another architecture which distributes and schedules the functionality across different clock cycles.

Table 1 and 2 show two possible architectures for example 2.1. Table 1 implies an architecture where all the three operations occur in the same clock cycle. Table 2 on the other hand, shows an architecture where the three operations are distributed across three clock cycles. Thus, the

Table 1: Architecture 1

Cycle #	Mult	Mult	Sub
1	*	*	-

Table 2: Architecture 2

Cycle #	Mult	Sub
1	*	
2	*	
3		-

multiplication "*" operations in Table 2 can be shared with a single hardware multiplier resource since they occur in different clock cycles.

2.2 Behavioral Synthesis Based ASIC Design Flow

Behavioral synthesis, as described in section 2.1, requires design description in either VHDL or Verilog HDL. Behavioral HDL can be manually described or can be generated automatically using commercial software tools such as Signal Processing Workbench (SPW) tool from Cadence Design Systems. SPW helps build behavioral block diagrams from system-level libraries. These include scalar, vector, and complex mathematical libraries that can generate behavioral HDL that feeds into behavioral synthesis tools.

Tight links between behavioral synthesis and logic synthesis tools is extremely desirable. Firstly, it allows dynamic calculations of timing and area for different operations. In other words, tight links with logic synthesis ensures that the behavioral synthesis tool would have access to critical timing and area information when making different trade-offs. Secondly, behavioral synthesis is essentially synthesis at a higher level of abstraction. In other words, behavioral synthesis is essentially a pre-logic synthesis step. Further, since the actual process of mapping a design to gates occurs during logic synthesis, a tight link between these tools helps in getting consistent results throughout the design flow. Besides, the behavioral HDL code, the other constraints or information required for behavioral synthesis tools include clock specifications, technology information, clock latency goals, wire-load models (at this stage the wire load models are however likely to be far from accurate) and operating conditions.

The primary objective of behavioral synthesis is to generate multiple functionally equivalent architectures with different timing and area characteristics. While the specific terminology and command flow are certain to differ from one commercial behavioral synthesis tools to another, conceptually, the flow can be characterized by a series of steps as shown in Figure 2.1. All the steps shown within the behavioral synthesis box in the figure are performed by the behavioral synthesis tool by execution of one or more commands depending on the behavioral synthesis tool used. The first step in the flow involves building of a graph based on the desired algorithm. The intent is to describe all data and control dependencies as well as any cycle restrictions that exist. The graph can be built for a minimum number of

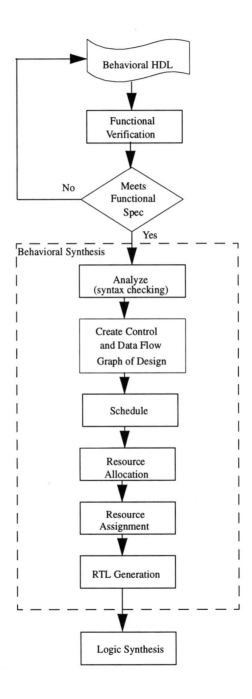

Figure 2.1 Behavioral Synthesis Flow

cycles (i.e. as soon as possible) or for minimum area. In other words, the user has a choice between targeting greater latency or lesser number of hardware resources.

The next step in behavioral synthesis is called Scheduling. It is the main step in behavioral synthesis and is analogous to the "compile" phase in logic synthesis when using the Synopsys Design Compiler. During this phase the operations in the design algorithm are assigned to specific clock cycles. Scheduling takes into account both the timing delays of the operations as well as the area of the resources that execute these operations but does not consider any wire load model information. Based on this information, the behavioral synthesis tool generates a design architecture with minimum latency or minimum hardware resources. If the user specifies any additional constraints prior to scheduling, then, these are also used to drive the scheduling process. Possible user-specified constraints include minimum or maximum number of cycles between operations, selection of pipelining the algorithm, mapping of arrays to ASIC vendor hard macro memory structures, latency, throughput, target technology etc.

Scheduling is followed by resource allocation and resource assignment. The resource allocation step involves identifying hardware resources for specific operations that have been scheduled. Resource assignment on the other hand, involves decisions about sharing (discussed in greater detail in section 2.4) of hardware resources among operations. Typically, sharing of hardware resources occurs in mutually exclusive clock cycles as well as mutually exclusive datapath streams. As the last step in behavioral synthesis, the worst case critical path is predicted and the RTL description of the design is written out from the behavioral synthesis tool. This RTL description is used for verification as well as logic synthesis.

The RTL code from behavioral synthesis tools are ASCII files but as with most machine generated code, is hard to read. Typically, the synthesized design from behavioral synthesis consists of a control unit, a datapath unit and memory. The control unit is a Mealy state machine which generates control signals to activate the different operations in specific clock cycles. The datapath unit consists of instantiation of datapath components such as multipliers, adders, incrementers and multiplexors.

2.3 Behavioral Synthesis Features

In this section, we describe the different salient features of behavioral synthesis including Operation chaining, Resource sharing, Inference of Sequential [Pipelined] Multi-cycle components, Memory inferencing, Register Lifetime Analysis, Automatic Pipelining, Behavioral Re-timing and Rolling and unrolling of for loops. Examples have been provided in the appropriate sections in order to illustrate the concepts.

2.3.1 Operation Chaining

An Operation is said to be "chained" when more than one operation is performed sequentially in the same clock cycle. Behavioral Synthesis tools are capable of automatically chaining operations in a clock cycle based on the clock period information and the timing delays of the operations. In other words, the behavioral synthesis tool implements multiple data dependent operations in the same clock cycle provided the total delay does not exceed the desired clock period.

Example 2.2   Logic to Perform Summation

```
z = a + b + c + d
y1= a+b /* 10 ns opeation*/
y2= y1+c /* 5 ns operation*/
z = y2+d /* 5 ns operation*/
```

Example 2.2 shows a simple summation of four variables a, b, c and d. The result z, is also shown as an outcome of three sequential operations of 10ns, 5ns and 5 ns each. Assuming a clock period of 25 ns, the behavioral synthesis tool automatically chains the above three operations into a single clock cycle. In general, greater the chaining of operations, lesser the sharing of resources. However, when considering multi-bit operations for chaining, bit-wise timing information for the operations should be used. Instead, if absolute summation of worst-case timing of components is used, it is likely to generate conservative results and impact the latency results of the behavioral synthesis tool. This is because it is often possible to accurately estimate timing delay of components by mathematical manipulation of bit-wise summation operations.

2.3.2   Resource Sharing

Resource sharing is defined as using the same hardware component resource to implement multiple arithmetic operations. Logic synthesis tools perform resource sharing of hardware components only in mutually exclusive branches within the same clock cycle as shown in Figure 2.2. The "+" is shared between the operation "B+D" and "A+C" only because they are in the same clock cycle.

Behavioral synthesis on the other hand can also perform resource sharing across clock cycles. In other words, it can re-use hardware resources scheduled for mutually exclusive clock cycles as well as mutually exclusive operations within the same clock cycle.

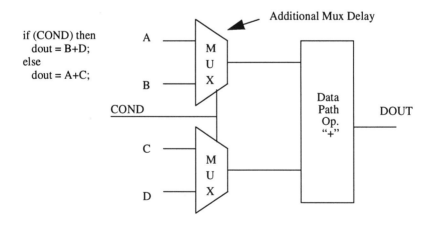

Figure 2.2 Resource Sharing in Logic Synthesis

Table 3: Resource sharing in Behavioral Synthesis

Clock Cycle	Addition
n	op1
n+1	
n+2	op2

In Table 3, operations op1 and op2 are identical operations which occur in different clock cycles. Behavioral synthesis tools interpret this to imply that the resource that performs this operation can be potentially shared. The main impact of resource sharing is the additional delay due to the multiplexors used for sharing of resources. In situations where the mux overhead exceeds the hardware resource overhead, resource sharing is not useful. Hence, behavioral synthesis tools perform a trade-off analysis when performing resource allocation.

2.3.3   Inference of Sequential (Pipelined) Multi-cycle components

Combinational multi-cycle components are components whose maximum timing delay exceeds the specified clock period. Sequential multi-cycle components are components with pipeline stages and hence require more than one cycle to execute based on the number of pipelined stages. Logic synthesis tools do not infer combinational and sequential multi-cycle components. However, logic synthesis tools allow the user to specify path exception commands to identify multi-cycle paths. Logic synthesis tools infer sequential components such as edge triggered flip-flops and level sensitive latches but do not infer memories and pipelined datapath components. Instead, they need to be instantiated in the HDL description.

Behavioral synthesis can infer both combinational and sequential multi-cycle components. If the delay of a component exceeds the specified clock period, behavioral synthesis automatically interprets it as a multi-cycle component of the required number of clock cycles and ensures that the input data is held stable for the required number of clock cycles. The main advantage of pipelined components over combinational multi-cycle components is the improved latency. This is because pipelined components help initiate multiple operations in a cascaded manner on the same pipelined hardware resource.

2.3.4   Memory Inferencing

In a typical logic synthesis approach, hard macros provided from the technology library such as memories are instantiated in the RTL code. Also, the state machine and the control logic of the design are explicitly described in the HDL.

In behavioral synthesis, the memory inferencing feature helps infer memory hard macros from the technology library for single and multi-dimensional array variables in the HDL code. Variable reads and writes in the HDL are scheduled as memory read and write operations. The memory timing, the number of ports, synchronous/asynchronous characteristics, combinational outputs etc. are modeled in the technology library. When the user chooses to map an array to a specific memory in the library during scheduling, the behavioral synthesis tool schedules the appropriate reads and writes and ensures automatic synthesis of the control logic. This is a very powerful feature of behavioral synthesis because it allows the system designer to explore and evaluate the design architecture using different memories.

2.3.5   Register Lifetime Analysis

Sequential register optimization is defined as analyzing the lifetimes of variables in a design and re-using registers for data values whose lifetimes do not overlap. In logic synthesis the inference of registers is defined in the RTL and these registers are never optimized during the logic synthesis process. Besides, sharing of registers in RTL is extremely complicated and impractical. It requires specific knowledge of "which data is held in what cycle". The re-using of registers for data values which are valid in mutually exclusive cycles causes an additional mux delay to be incurred. The behavioral synthesis tool takes into account the impact of the delay due to the additional mux when considering register sharing on critical timing paths.

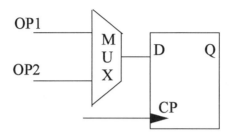

Figure 2.3 Register Sharing

In Figure 2.3, OP1 and OP2 are operation values generated in mutually exclusive clock cycles, and hence share the same register. Lifetime analysis of registers in behavioral synthesis is a distinct advantage over logic synthesis and can result in significant area improvement.

2.3.6   Automatic Pipelining

Pipelining an algorithm is a technique that ensures that the next iteration of the algorithm begins execution before the current iteration completes. The following two terms are commonly used during pipelining, namely, *initiation rate* and *latency*. Initiation rate or throughput is defined as the rate at which the input arrives. "Latency" is defined as the total number of cycles for one iteration of the algorithm to complete. Implementing pipelining in RTL is extremely complicated. Further, the RTL needs to be re-written for different throughput and latency requirements. Behavioral synthesis on the other hand is capable of automatic pipelining.

Example 2.3   Loop Algorithm

```
count:= 0;
algo: while (count < 15) loop
    vara := read input;
    varb := read input;
--computation based on vara and varb
--write out results;
```

```
    count := count + 1;
end loop; -- algo
```

Example 2.3 shows a sample behavioral code with a while loop. Let us assume that one iteration of the loop above takes 20 cycles to complete. Hence, five iterations of this algorithm will take 100 clock cycles. If new inputs can be made available every 5 cycles then we can potentially start a new iteration of the algorithm every 5 cycles. i.e., initiation interval or throughput of 5.

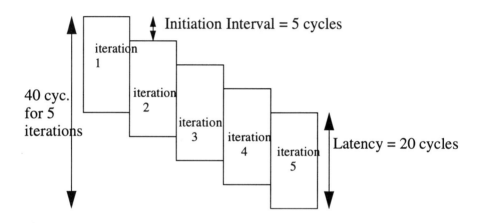

Figure 2.4 Pipeline to Reduce Throughput

Thus, the number of cycles to complete 5 iterations of the algorithm will be

```
20 (for first iteration) + 4 (# of remaining iterations) x
5(initiation interval) = 40 clock cycles.
```

as shown in Figure 2.4. Hence, there is an improvement in the overall latency of the algorithm. However, this improvement can be at the cost of substantial hardware resources i.e. more area. Besides, pipelining can only be considered if there are no preventing data dependencies from one iteration to the next and new sets of data are available to support it. In general, pipelining a design algorithm is most useful under the following scenarios:

High Data Throughput Requirements: When the system requirement dictates high data processing throughput pipelining is required.

Different Types of Operations: If the algorithm consists of using different types of operations i.e. multipliers, adders etc., then the area overhead of pipelining is not as significant, since it is likely that hardware resources that are unused for many cycles already exist in the design. In such cases, pipelining a design will result in latency advantages without the associated area overhead.

Speed Critical: Pipelining can be considered for design applications where speed is the major consideration over area. e.g., microprocessors.

2.3.7   Rolling and Unrolling of *For* Loops

Unrolling a *for* loop is defined as opening all the iterations of the loop and executing them in parallel. Keeping a *for* loop rolled implies performing the iterations of the loop sequentially. The advantage to unrolling a *for* loop is the improved latency over a rolled *for* loop. On the other hand, the *for* loop when rolled results in smaller area but higher latency. This is because the iterations of the loop are performed sequentially and hence can result in greater resource sharing. Further, the *for* loop when rolled reduces the complexity of the scheduling process.

Logic synthesis tools unlike behavioral synthesis tools, do not provide the flexibility to choose the mode of implementation of the *for* loops. They are always unrolled during logic synthesis.

Example 2.4   Rolling and Unrolling of for loops.

```
algo_loop: for i in 0 to 99 loop
sum = sum + coef(i) * shiftreg(i);
end loop;
```

Example 2.4 shows the HDL description of a *for* loop, with two operations "+" and "*" for each iteration of the loop. When this *for* loop is unrolled, there will be 200 operations to be scheduled and potentially greater than two hardware resources required. But the algorithm can be executed in fewer clock cycles. On the other hand, if the *for* loop is kept rolled, then, the complexity of scheduling is reduced to two operations and a counter that loops from 0 to 99. However, the algorithm would take more cycles to complete since the iterations are performed in a serial fashion. In some cases, unrolling *for* loops does not speed up the design due to other bottlenecks such as memory access etc.

2.3.8   Behavioral Re-Timing

Behavioral re-timing (BRT) is defined as optimization of registers or moving of registers across logic boundaries to meet timing constraints and reduce register cost. BRT works on a gate level netlist (prior to scan insertion) and optimizes a design by balancing the combinational logic between registers. Thus, although a feature of behavioral synthesis tools, BRT is post-logic synthesis step.

In general, designs consist of tight critical timing paths and slack paths. It is very difficult problem for a designer to code a design such that combinational delays between registers are equal. Hence, BRT provides this automatic capability. This capability re-times the design without changing the functionality at the ASIC boundaries or at the interface. However, internal to the design, cycle to cycle functionality at the register points will undergo changes after BRT. This can be an issue when the verification methodology involves probing of internal register points. The advantage of this approach lies in that it is an automatic way of improving the timing of the design at the gate level.

Figure 2.5a shows a design with clock period of 20 ns where the combinational delay between the first two registers is 6ns, while that between the next two registers is 21ns. Figure 2.5b shows the same design after BRT with combinational delays re-distributed between the register sets such that the delay between the first set of registers is 12ns, while the delay between the next set of registers is 15 ns. In other words, BRT has been successfully applied to the design to meet the required clock period of 20ns.

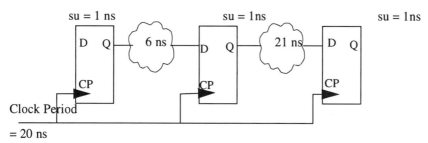

Figure 2-5a Design Before Behavioral Re-timing

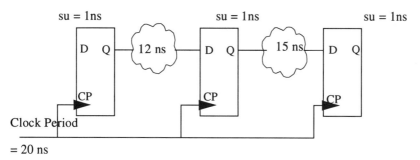

Figure 2-5b Design After Behavioral Re-timing

Figure 2.5 Behavioral Re-timing

Other applications of BRT are when creating pipelined versions of user-specified functions. For example, when user created combinational functions do not complete in one clock cycle, then pipeline stages can be added to the design automatically using this capability. Though BRT is run at the gate level, it is often classified as a behavioral synthesis based optimization because of the sequential optimization algorithms that are used.

Figure 2.6 and Figure 2.7 show another application of BRT techniques. Notice that there is a reduction in the number of registers used after BRT without any change in the functionality.

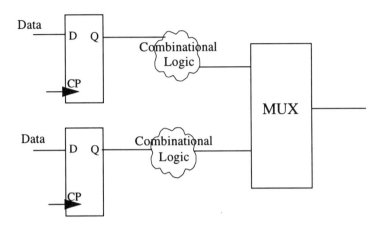

Figure 2.6 Design Before BRT

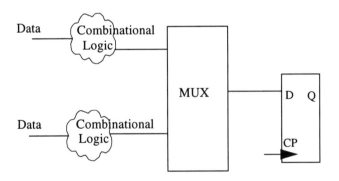

Figure 2.7 Design After BRT

2.4 The Transition to Behavioral Synthesis

Behavioral synthesis is an exciting technology that has many advantages and can significantly boost designer productivity. As discussed in previous sections in this chapter, the coding style for behavioral synthesis is different from that for conventional logic synthesis and involves a significant learning curve. Porting the same RTL code to a newer technology using logic synthesis does not necessarily take full advantage of the new technology. But behavioral synthesis which is intended for architectural exploration can take advantage of the new technology since it is deployed at a higher level of abstraction. In other words, a different architecture could prove more beneficial in a newer technology. Tight integration between behavioral synthesis and logic synthesis as well as physical domain tools is critical. Without this integration, the convergence of timing at the pre and post placement stages can result in several iterations between behavioral synthesis and downstream tools.

In short, like any new technology or design methodology, the move to behavioral synthesis has its own share of challenges. In this section, we cover issues which need to be considered when adopting the behavioral synthesis.

2.4.1   Design Partitioning

An effective partitioning strategy for RTL synthesis after behavioral synthesis is critical to achieving an optimal netlist after logic synthesis. Typically, behavioral synthesis tools consider complexity in terms of number of operations. Behavioral synthesis generates RTL code which consists of a state machine (FSM) and an instantiation of datapath operation components. It is possible that behavioral synthesis tools generate RTL designs exceeding 200K gates. However, logic synthesis tools are incapable of handling such large designs. Thus, partitioning techniques are critical. One approach is to use a datapath synthesis software to synthesize the datapath components and use conventional logic synthesis tools for synthesizing the state machine. However, integrating these datapath components from datapath synthesis tools into the design could pose a new set of challenges.

2.4.2   Verification

Another critical issue when migrating to a behavioral synthesis based design flow is the verification strategy. At the behavioral HDL level there is no concept of timing i.e. no clock cycles are defined. At the RTL level, however, (generated automatically from behavioral synthesis), this timing information has been incorporated. Since the same testbenches need to be used at the Behavioral and RTL level, handshaking protocols/strategies need to be implemented to ensure that the verification is consistent both at the behavioral and at the RTL level.

2.4.3   Power Reduction

With increasing sizes of designs and the need for low power applications, power is another optimization constraint that has become critical in addition to timing and area. The Power Compiler from Synopsys is an example of a tool that performs logic optimization on the RTL to meet power constraints. As behavioral synthesis tools gain in usage, power reduction capabilities at the behavioral level will be a big plus. However, this requires the modeling of power information for all cells in the technology library. This feature in behavioral synthesis tools in conjunction with gate-level power analysis tools such as Design Power from Synopsys can help achieve effective lower power implementations of designs. Since power analysis tools are dependent on the data switching activity information, some worst case estimates can be taken for analysis purposes. Finally, traditional power saving techniques like clock gating as well as reducing the activity on the datapath logic are also being implemented in behavioral synthesis tools. Also, power estimation tools (e.g., Wattwatcher from Sente Inc.) can be used after behavioral synthesis on the RTL generated for the design.

2.4.4   Guidelines for Behavioral Synthesis

1. The HDL constructs supported for Behavioral Synthesis are the same as those supported for Logic Synthesis.

2. The same HDL constructs are interpreted differently by both Behavioral synthesis and Logic synthesis tools.

3. Behavioral synthesis tools support only one clock in the design as well as only one edge of the clock.

4. Synchronous and asynchronous reset styles are supported. This capability allows the user to model the system reset behavior.

5. In general, all inputs to behavioral designs are assumed to be registered while all outputs are automatically registered.

6. Logic synthesis does not permit *for* loops to contain clock edge statements (i.e. `wait` and `@posedge`). This is possible in behavioral designs, since behavioral synthesis is capable of generating a state machine and separate datapath logic.

7. Behavioral synthesis tools have the capability to keep for loops rolled or unrolled. When a *for* loop remains "rolled", a counter and a comparator are inferred.

8. In behavioral designs, combinational multi-cycle operations can be inferred and resource shared automatically whereas in logic synthesis this is not possible.

Lastly, the mechanism for passing of information from behavioral synthesis to downstream logic synthesis tools must be considered. In addition, to the RTL code written out from behavioral synthesis, some of the other information which needs to be passed down to logic synthesis includes list of multi-cycle operations, sequential pipelined components, implementation selection of arithmetic components, any functional false paths created etc. The behavioral synthesis tool must be capable of writing this constraint information for the logic synthesis tool to use during synthesis. Thus, tight links with the logic synthesis tools is imperative in order to ensure smooth transfer of information.

2.5 Infinite Impulse Response Filter

Infinite Impulse Response (IIR) filters are a category of digital filters that can be characterized in time by a difference equation and in the frequency domain by Z transform. Digital filters are implemented in hardware using adders, delay elements and multipliers. IIR filters are also known as recursive or Auto-Regressive Moving Average filters.

The algorithm for an IIR is represented by

```
y(n) = b0x(n) + b1x(n-1) + b2x(n-2) +.. + bNx(n-N) + a1y(n-1) +
a2y(n-2)+... + aNy(n-N)
```

where x(n) is the nth input sample of data;

x(n-1) the (n-1)th sample and so on.

"b0, b1.." and "a1, a2.." are the coefficients of the filter.

An IIR filter is identified by the "order" of the filter and its coefficient values. The output of a N order IIR filter is dependent on "N" past responses of the filter and "N" previous input data samples. Hence, for a N-Order IIR there are (2N+1) coefficients. In hardware, this implies 2N+1 multipliers and 2N adders. In general, IIR filters are designed for specific latency and throughput goals. For example, the system specifications could require a throughput of 4 and a latency of 16. This means new data samples must be processed every 4 clock cycles and that the algorithm must be completed in 16 cycles. Thus, although the IIR is conceptually a basic building block that can be used in different applications, it has different throughput and latency requirements. In the RTL world, this implies describing the IIR each time, using different RTL architectures based on the desired latency and throughput goals.

In addition to the latency and throughput requirements, another variable for IIRs are the coefficients. For instance, the design might require that the coefficients be constant. In such cases, they can be hard coded in the HDL. Alternately, coefficients can be such that they are loaded by the system upon system reset. Another alternative is for the coefficients to be programmable and changed at regular intervals as in the case of an Adaptive Equalizer filter. Thus, the coefficients of the filter could either be hard-coded constants, or stored in a memory (RAM, ROM or in sequential registers) depending on the requirements of the algorithm. The storage of coefficients changes the access cycles and hence can have an impact on the overall latency of the design.

As mentioned earlier, behavioral synthesis generates multiple RTL architectures using the same behavioral code. Thus, design scenarios such as those described above are ideal for behavioral synthesis, since they fundamentally involve identifying a specific architecture based on a series of trade-offs. Described in this section is a basic model of an IIR filter. It can quite easily be adapted to generate handshaking signals for the IO protocol. The issue of quantization of data has not been incorporated in the design. This can be addressed by creating subprograms for the different quantization algorithms (such as clipping, rounding, ceiling, floor etc.) and appropriately using them in the behavioral description of the design. In short, the intent in Example 2.5 is to provide a sample Behavioral description for a design which can be re-designed for specific system applications.

Example 2.5   HDL Description of IIR Filter

```
--VHDL Behavioral Description
-- Infinite Impulse Response Filter
-- Recursive
-- N Order Filter
-- 2N+1 coefficients
-- y(n) = b0x(n) + b1x(n-1) + b2x(n-2) +... + bNx(n-N)
-- + a1y(n-1) + ---a2y(n-2)+... + aNy(n-N)
-- 2nd order (N=2) 5 filter coefficients
-- For a N Order IIR there are (2N+1) coefficients and
-- hence 2N+1 multipliers and 2N adders.


library IEEE;
use IEEE.std_logic_1164.all;
use IEEE.std_logic_arith.all;

entity IIR1 is
   generic ( order: natural:= 6;
               data_width: natural:= 8;
               coeff_width: natural:= 10;
               count: natural:= 5; -- # of iterations before
                                   -- updating coefficients
               filterout_width : natural := 12);
   port ( clk: in std_logic;
           reset: in std_logic;
           enable: in std_logic;
           coeffin: in signed(coeff_width - 1 downto 0);
           datain: in signed(data_width - 1 downto 0);
           data_available: out std_logic;
           new_coeff: out std_logic;
           filterout: out signed((filterout_width - 1) downto 0));
end IIR1;


architecture BEHAVE of IIR1 is
```

```
begin
P1: process
-- Defining the coefficient array structure
    subtype coeff_word is signed(coeff_width-1 downto 0);
    type coeff_array is array((2*order+1)-1 downto 0)
                                                of coeff_word;
    variable coeff_prog: coeff_array;
-- Defining the array structure for the past responses
    subtype past_resp_word is signed(filterout_width - 1 downto
0);
    type past_resp_array is array(order-1 downto 0) of
past_resp_word;
    variable past_resp_reg: past_resp_array;
--:= past_resp_array'(others => past_resp_word'(others =>'0'));


-- Defining the array structure for the input samples
  subtype data_word is signed(data_width - 1 downto 0);
  type data_array is array((order+1)-1 downto 0) of data_word;
  variable data_reg : data_array;
--:= data_array'(others => data_word'(others => '0'));


    subtype sop_word is signed((filterout_width + coeff_width -
1) downto 0);
    subtype sop1_word is signed((data_width + coeff_width -
1)downto 0);


    subtype sop2_word is signed((filterout_width + coeff_width -
1) downto 0);
    variable sop : sop_word;
    variable sop1 : sop1_word;
    variable sop2 : sop2_word;

begin
  main_loop : loop
    -- initialize the coefficients
    wait on clk until clk = '1';
    -- added for behavioral simulation
    load_coeff: for i in 2*order downto 0 loop
                coeff_prog(i):= coeffin;
```

```
     wait on clk until clk = '1';
     end loop;
     new_coeff <= '0';
     wait on clk until clk = '1';
       filter: for i in count - 1 downto 0 loop
       hshk_loop: while (enable = '0') loop
         wait on clk until clk = '1';
       end loop;

-- Shifter operation
shift_loop: for i in order downto 1 loop -- N + 1
     data_reg(i) := data_reg(i-1);
end loop;

data_reg(0) := datain; -- IO Read
-- Initialize sum of products accumulation
-- Currently aggregates not supported
-- sop := sop_word'(others => '0');

sop1 := conv_signed(0, data_width + coeff_width);
sop_loop1: for i in (order) downto 0 loop
     sop1 := sop1 + data_reg(i) * coeff_prog(i);
             wait on clk until clk = '1';
end loop;

sop2 := conv_signed(0, filterout_width + coeff_width);
sop_loop2: for i in (order-1) downto 0 loop
     sop2 := sop2 + past_resp_reg(i) * coeff_prog(i + order + 1);
     wait on clk until clk = '1';
end loop;

sop := sop1 + sop2;
past_loop: for i in (order-1) downto 1 loop
     past_resp_reg(i) := past_resp_reg(i-1);
end loop;
     past_resp_reg(0) := sop(filterout_width-1 downto 0);
     data_available <= '1';
     filterout <= sop(filterout_width-1 downto 0);
     wait on clk until clk = '1';
```

```
    data_available <= '0';
    wait on clk until clk = '1';
    end loop; -- filter loop
    new_coeff <= '1';
  end loop; -- main loop
end process;
end BEHAVE;
```

-- Verilog Behavioral Description
```verilog
module IIR (clk, reset, enable, coeffin, datain,
        data_available, new_coeff, filterout);
parameter order=6;
parameter data_width=8;
parameter coeff_width=10;
parameter count=5;
parameter filterout_width=12;

// Port declarations in Verilog
input clk, reset, enable;
input[coeff_width-1:0] coeffin;
input[data_width-1:0] datain;
output data_available, new_coeff;
output[filterout_width-1:0] filterout;

// Registered outputs
reg data_available, new_coeff;
reg [filterout_width-1:0] filterout;
// used for for loops
integer i;

/* Defining the coefficient array structure */
reg [coeff_width-1:0] coeff_prog [(2*order+1)-1:0];
/* Defining the array structure for the past responses */
reg [filterout_width-1:0] past_resp_reg [order-1:0];
/* Defining the array structure for the input samples */
reg [data_width-1:0] data_reg [(order+1)-1:0];
reg [(filterout_width +coeff_width)-1:0] sop;
reg [(data_width + coeff_width) - 1:0] sop1;
```

```verilog
reg [(filterout_width + coeff_width)-1:0] sop2;

always
   begin
      forever
         begin
//initialize the coefficients
         @ (posedge clk);
         for (i = 2*order; i >= 0; i = i - 1)
         begin
            coeff_prog[i] = coeffin;
            @(posedge clk);
         end
         new_coeff = 0;
         @(posedge clk);

// filter loop
         for(i = count-1; i >=0; i = i - 1)
         begin
            while(!enable)
            begin
               @(posedge clk);
            end
   // shifter operation
            for(i = order-1; i >= 1; i = i - 1)
            begin
               data_reg[i] = data_reg[i-1];
            end
            data_reg[0] = datain;   //IO Read
   //sop_loop1
            sop1 = 0;
            for(i = order; i >= 0; i = i - 1)
            begin
               sop1 = sop1 + data_reg[i]*coeff_prog[i];
               @(posedge clk);
            end
   //sop_loop2
            sop2=0;
            for(i = order-1; i >= 0; i = i - 1)
```

```
            begin
              sop2 = sop2 + past_resp_reg[i]*coeff_prog[i + order
+ 1];
                @(posedge clk);
            end
            sop = sop1 + sop2;
   //past_loop
            for(i = order-1; i >= 1; i = i - 1)
            begin
               past_resp_reg[i] = past_resp_reg[i-1];
            end
            past_resp_reg[0] = sop[filterout_width - 1:0];
            data_available = 1;
            filterout = sop[filterout_width-1:0];
            @(posedge clk);
            data_available = 0;
            @(posedge clk);
            end // forever
      new_coeff = 1;
      end // forever
   end     // always
endmodule
```

2.6 Methodology Audit

The intent of the methodology audit is to assist designers and CAD engineers to take a snapshot of their current design methodologies and investigate the need for appropriate changes. In this section, the audit is relevant to all current or future users of behavioral synthesis.

1. Is your design partitioned by clock domain? Note that behavioral synthesis supports only one clock domain and one clock edge.

2. Have you considered the trade-offs involved in implementation of arrays in registers as opposed to using embedded memories? When using embedded memories, behavioral synthesis is capable of directly mapping to memories from the library.

3. Do you take special care to ensure that the HDL code has been partitioned effectively in order to take maximum advantage of behavioral synthesis features such as resource sharing, operation chaining,

memory inferencing etc. Note that behavioral synthesis performs resource sharing and optimal parallel scheduling of operations only within the same HDL block.

4. Have you considered issues such as increasing the clock speed at the expense of more cycles? Contributing factors include resource sharing, higher bandwidth, faster RAMs etc.

5. Has the design been partitioned to minimize handshaking protocol overhead between blocks? Behavioral Synthesis implicitly understands the control flow and dependency within a block.

6. Does the methodology consider integration of custom blocks such as MACs, CAMs etc.?

7. When the design requires pipelining, do you follow a specific coding style? Throughput requirements of design can dictate pipelining of design. Issues such as handling of flushing and stalling the pipeline also need to be considered.

8. If your design is timing critical, have you considered transformations such as Carry Save Adders for arithmetic operations?

9. Are you making use of behavioral re-timing (BRT) techniques? This can be used to improve the timing of the design after the netlist has been generated.

10. Have you taken care to ensure that the same testbench can be used both at the behavioral and the RTL level?

CHAPTER 3 — *Verification Methodology*

As the design traverses through different levels of abstraction (RTL, pre-layout netlist, post-scan insertion netlist, post-layout netlist etc.) in the design flow it is essential to verify that the functionality and the timing goals of the design are met at each stage. Further, when the chip design nears completion, it often undergoes minor changes ("tweaking") like buffer up-sizing and down-sizing, to meet timing goals. These tweaks typically result in small or no changes in the logic functionality of the chip. However, it is required to verify the design after it has undergone any changes. In general, because of the large size of the designs, verifying the design at different stages in the design flow can require long, computationally expensive simulation regression tests. Moreover, with the advent of deep sub-micron technologies, it is essential to verify the design with accurate interconnect resistance and capacitance. Thus, with increasing design sizes and the advent of deep sub-micron technologies, the task of design verification poses serious challenges.

In this chapter, we discuss HDL simulation in general, various types of simulators and their applications, and the limitations of conventional simulation methodology. Finally, we discuss emerging design verification methodologies such as cycle based simulation and formal verification and propose a strategy for migrating to these methodologies.

This chapter is organized as follows. The first section explores the different levels of abstraction as the design traverses through the flow, namely, behavioral, RTL, gate-level, and layout. It also discusses the role of static timing analysis and simulation in the design process. The next section classifies logic simulators into various categories and discusses different simulators. It also describes the distinction between event-driven and cycle-based simulators, compiled-code versus interpreted code simulators and techniques for developing simulation testplan and testbenches. Following this, we discuss interfaces to simulators that are used in different applications. This section covers topics like interfaces to foreign languages (C, C++), hardware accelerators, hardware/software models, mixed VHDL/Verilog simulators and mixed signal (analog/digital) simulators. The last three sections cover simulation and verification technologies including cycle-based simulation and formal verification. Finally, a strategy to migrate to the next generation simulation technology is discussed.

3.1 Verification at Different Levels of Abstraction

A typical ASIC design process involves several levels of abstraction. In other words, it is possible to describe a design using flow charts, state diagrams, high-level hardware description languages etc. The goal of verification is to ensure that the design meets its functional and timing requirements at each of these different levels of abstraction. In general, this process consists of the following conceptual steps:

1. Creating the design at a higher level of abstraction
2. Verifying the design at that level of abstraction
3. Translating the design to a lower level of abstraction
4. Verifying the consistency between steps 1 and 3
5. Steps 2, 3, and 4 are repeated until tapeout.

Figure 3.1 illustrates the design at different levels of abstraction. The verification methodology applied at each stage of the design process is specified in the figure.

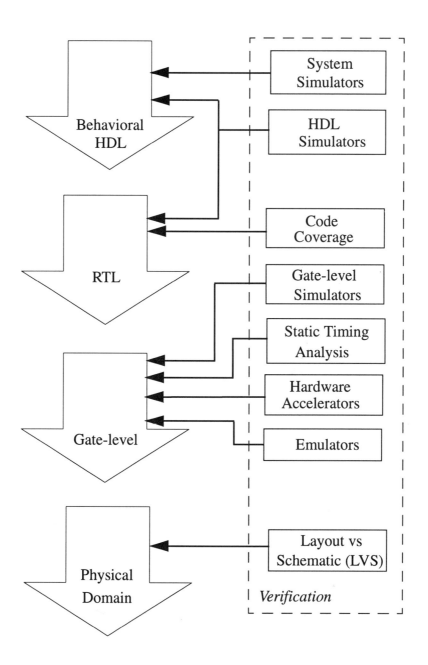

Figure 3.1 Levels of Abstraction in Digital Design Flow

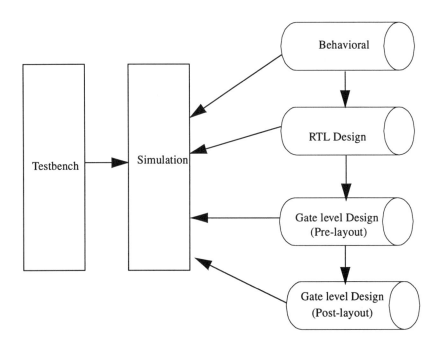

Figure 3.2 Simulation using the same testbench

Digital logic simulation is one approach to verify the design at different levels of abstraction. In order to maintain consistency, the same testbench must be used for simulation at each level of abstraction as shown in Figure 3.2.

3.1.1   Behavioral Simulation

Behavioral simulation is a widely used term and can be easily mis-interpreted. In this book, we refer to behavioral simulation to imply simulation of HDL in which, the clock cycle to clock cycle activity is not defined. The behavioral HDL description is different from conventional RTL code. The design is initially described at the behavioral level to verify the concept and basic functionality. In other words, it is the design intent that is captured at a high-level, rather than the specifics of the implementation. At this stage, the design can be specified using Hardware Description Languages (HDL) like VHDL and Verilog for use with commercial simulators such as Leapfrog, V-System, NC-Verilog, VCS etc. For special purpose applications like Digital Signal Processing (DSP), the design can also be specified using schematic capture for system simulators like SPW, COSSAP etc. Behavioral synthesis is then performed on this design to optimize the design at architectural level with constraints for clock, latency, and throughput. The output of behavioral synthesis is an RTL level design, with clocks, registers, and buses. Behavioral synthesis is yet to be widely adopted for several reasons including—behavioral synthesis requires a HDL coding style that is different from conventional RTL coding styles, lack of complete control over the architecture inferred in RTL, the quality of results when compared to RTL designs, the need for purely synchronous designs, restrictions on number of clocks supported etc. Hence, most designs are still described at the RTL level.

3.1.2   RTL Simulation

Most designs are described in an ASCII format using the synthesizable subset of the VHDL and Verilog language. This synthesizable subset is referred to as Register Transfer Level (RTL). For certain applications like state machines, graphical tools are available the generate VHDL and Verilog descriptions. The RTL design is simulated to verify functionality. The architecture and coding styles used in the RTL code significantly influence the area and timing of the synthesized design. Once the RTL code has been simulated and analyzed, it is ready for logic synthesis.

3.1.3   Static Timing Analysis

Once the gate-level netlist has been generated, the next step is to verify the timing of the design. Static Timing Analysis is a technique used to verify the timing characteristics of a design. This approach is well-suited to synchronous designs. Typically, RTL when synthesized generates synchronous logic with simple clock structures. Thus, logic synthesis and static timing analysis tools are complementary technologies. Logic synthesis tools are well-integrated with static timing analysis tools. For example, the DesignTime static timing analysis tool from Synopsys is well-integrated with the Synopsys Design Compiler.

Static timing analysis does not require any test vectors. The inputs to a static timing analysis tool include the netlist, library models of the cells in the technology library (the timing arcs in the technology library are critical but it ignores the functionality of the cells) and constraints such as clock period, waveform, skews, false paths, input and output delays for blocks, drive for inputs and load on outputs and multi-cycle paths. Using this information the static timing analysis tool, calculates the delay through the combinational logic, the setup and hold time of the registers and identifies "slack" in all paths in the design. Static timing analysis verifies timing of the design, typically in a fraction of the time it would take for logic simulation. Further, it exhaustively checks every possible path in the design without the need for test vectors. However, it does not ensure functional correctness of the design. For example, if an "and" function were used in place of an "or" function in the design, static timing analysis will not be able to identify this error. Chapter 5 discusses static timing analysis in detail.

3.1.4   Gate-level Simulation (pre-layout)

Simulation is performed on the synthesized gate-level netlist prior to placement and routing for two main purposes. Firstly, to ensure that the design functionality before and after synthesis is identical. It is possible that the RTL description does not completely describe the required functionality. Alternately, it is also possible that specific controls required to be applied to guide the synthesis tool in order to generate the desired implementation. Secondly, to dynamically verify the timing of the design with cell delays from the target technology library and estimated wire delays for interconnects. This technique used for timing verification is different from a static timing approach. Gate-level simulation is performed both at the module level and as well as at the chip level depending on the verification environment used for a design. Unit delay functional gate-level simulation can also be used to verify functionality of the design.

3.1.5   Gate-Level Simulation (post-layout)

As designs migrate to smaller geometries, interconnect delays constitute a larger portion of the overall delay. Hence, it is imperative that these delays are extracted and back-annotated on the design. It is possible to extract both resistance (R) and capacitance (C) for the design using RC extraction tools. The back-annotation can be in the form of a load script, a resistance script, the Standard Delay Format (SDF), the Detailed Standard Parasitic Format (DSPF) etc. After back-annotation data is available, static timing analysis and gate-level simulation are performed on the design to verify that the design still meets timing. The design is simulated after layout to ensure that timing is met with accurate interconnect delays (loads) from layout. This is different from the pre-layout simulation which involves verification using estimated loads.

3.2 Classification of Simulators

In this section, we describe the different kinds of simulators used at each stage of the verification process as the design traverses through different levels of abstraction. Logic simulators can be classified into the following categories as illustrated in Figure 3.3:

HDL-based Simulators: The design and testbench are described using HDL (Verilog, VHDL). Some examples of commercial tools include NC-Verilog, Leapfrog, V-System, VSS, VCS.

Schematic-based Simulators: The design is entered graphically using a schematic editor. Some examples include ViewDraw, Concept etc.

Emulators: The design is mapped into FPGA hardware for prototype simulation. Emulation is used to perform hardware/software co-simulation.

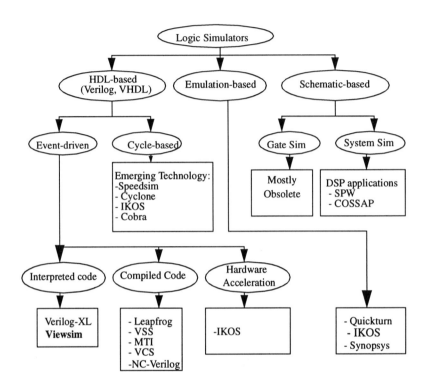

Figure 3.3 Classification of Simulators.

3.2.1   HDL-based Simulators

Simulators can be interpreted code, compiled code, or hardware accelerated. The distinction between each of these is discussed below and illustrated in Figure 3.4.

Interpreted Code Simulators: The HDL files are interpreted line-by-line by the simulator and stored in simulation memory instead of the hard disk. Thus, event driven simulation requires a long start-up time for each simulation even if the HDL code is unchanged.

Compiled code simulators: The HDL files in compiled code simulators, are compiled into intermediate binary file. One form of compiled code is to convert HDL files into intermediate format such as

"C" code, and then compile it using a "C" compiler. Another approach is to convert HDL files to machine code optimized for the target workstation's CPU architecture—these are referred to as native compiled code simulators. Compiled code simulators have short start-up time for each simulation run. In general, native compiled code simulators run faster than the C compiled code simulators. However, native compile code simulators are not easily portable to other platforms.

Hardware Accelerators: In this approach, simulation is done using hardware designed specifically for simulation purpose. This can provide speedup of 10-100x over software simulators for structural (gate-level) designs. The speed up in the simulation helps simulate the design with greater number of test vectors.

The HDL-based simulators can be classified as event-driven or cycle-based.

Event-driven simulators: In this approach to simulation, an event is defined by a change in logic value. Thus, a change on any node in the design causes the simulator to schedule events to evaluate the affected portion of the design in the fanout network of that node. Event-driven simulation technology is currently most heavily used and is well-suited for all types of designs.

Cycle-based simulators: Cycle-based simulators take advantage of the fact that most digital designs are largely synchronous. In synchronous circuits, state elements change their values on the active edge of clock. Therefore, by computing the steady state response of a circuit at each clock cycle, a speedup of 10x-100x over event-driven simulation can be achieved. However, cycle based simulators do have certain limitatioms. For instance, cycle based simulators can't detect glitching behavior. Section 3.5 and 3.6 describes cycle and event based simulation techniques and their pros and cons in greater detail.

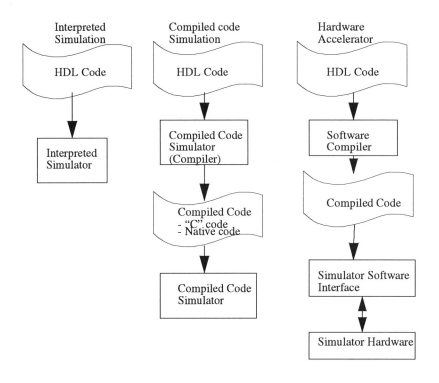

Figure 3.4 Interpreted, Compiled, and Hardware Simulators.

Cycle based simulators are not interpreted simulators. Instead, they use compiled algorithms which translate the circuits into machine executable code. Before any code is generated the circuit is levelized. Interpreted algorithms generate netlist and opcodes which are loaded in the data structures that drive the simulation engine (in other words it generates pseudo code for virtual machines).

3.2.2   Schematic-based simulators

The schematic based simulators can be used for gate-level simulations or system-level simulations as discussed below:

Gate-level simulators: With the increase in sizes of designs, schematic entry of designs is fast becoming obsolete. As a result schematic based gate level simulators are being replaced by HDL-based simulators.

System-level simulators: System level simulators assist the user to capture the design at the architectural level, using high-level library components (e.g. adders, multipliers etc.). The design can be represented in floating point initially, and fixed point (buses) later. The intent is to make possible simulation at the architectural level with the available library of components.

3.2.3 Emulation

Checking hardware and software compatibility early in the design cycle is critical, especially as design sizes increase and software gets more complex. Emulation provides an effective mechanism to verify this compatibility through fast prototyping. This "virtual" environment can be used to verify the functionality of the IC in its target system as well test the actual software that runs on the system (also known as hardware-software co-simulation). Appendix A lists a few of the commercial emulation tool vendors.

Emulators can run designs in a matter of hours as opposed to software simulators which may take several days. It can provide of the order of 1000x speedup over conventional event-driven simulation. Emulation involves running the simulation at relatively slow speeds of under 2 Mhz. Thus, emulation is not meant to accurately verify timing for an ASIC design which is targeted to a standard cell technology. This is especially true for deep sub-micron designs where interconnect delays dominate the cell delays and are heavily dependent on the target floorplanning and place and route tools. Emulation is an excellent methodology for hardware/software co-simulation, for prototype verification and identifying of functional bugs.

In the past, setting up a system for emulation took several weeks. However, this is begun to change with rapid improvements in emulation technology such as the custom processor-based, compiled code logic emulation systems, better debug capabilities, interfaces to conventional simulators etc. These systems make possible a compilation speed of upto one million gates per hour and an overall capacity as high as 8 million gates.

There are essentially two approaches to emulation—the custom board approach and the emulation board approach. The custom board approach involves configuring the design in an array of Field Programmable Gate Arrays (FPGAs). This implies developing a prototype of the ASIC that can fit into the actual target system. In the Emulation box approach, the ASIC netlist is directly translated to the target system without having to specifically target FPGAs as in the custom board approach. In other words, at the synthesis stage mapping to actual FPGAs is not performed. Instead the RTL is mapped to cells from the ASIC library. This ASIC netlist is the directly mapped to FPGAs external to the logic synthesis environment. The custom board approach is more time consuming since it requires synthesizing to FPGA libraries, followed by partitioning the design across multiple FPGAs. The latter approach on the other hand is far more expensive.

3.3 Developing Simulation Testplan and Testbenches

There are three basic aspects to the entire process of simulation. First, the process of writing test vectors. Second, the actual running of the simulation. Thirdly, inspecting the results of the simulation steps to ensure that the results of the simulation are indeed correct. A simulation testplan is intended to address all of these issues. A simulation testplan is created by developing testbenches and test patterns to cover every function of the design specification.

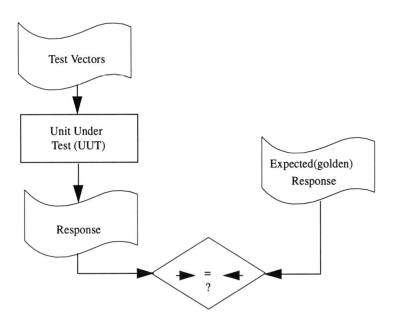

Figure 3.5 Basic Simulation Process.

Simulating a design involves applying a set of test vectors to the input ports of the design or the Unit Under Test (UUT) and comparing the response on the output ports with the golden expected response as shown in Figure 3.5. The limitation of this technique for setting up the testbench lies in that one has to manually verify and store the expected response for every simulation vector. Another technique is to apply random or deterministic test patterns simultaneously to two models of the design and compare the responses as illustrated in Figure 3.6. This technique avoids storing and verifying each expected response and is applicable to random patterns as well. However, it inherently assumes that one of the two models is the reference model, which functions correctly.

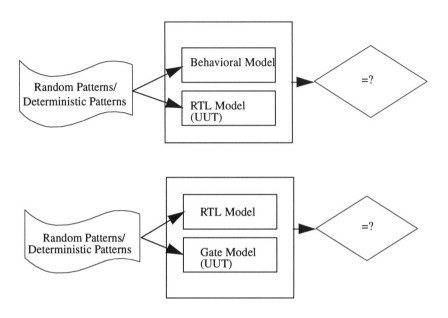

Figure 3.6 Testbench with two simulation models.

When creating a testbench, there are two ways for comparing the response with expected response:

1. Store the response from the UUT in a file and compare it against the golden (or reference) file: This technique does not provide diagnostics in case of simulation failure and cannot be used with random patterns.

2. Write self-checking code: Self-checking code is written using the HDL and is embedded in the testbench. It checks for incorrect functional or timing results during simulation and flags appropriate error message. This is the preferred technique for checking responses, because it can provide error diagnostics and reduce the debug time.

3.3.1   HDL Code Coverage

Code coverage tools [27] are used to determine which portions of the HDL (VHDL/Verilog) code did not get executed by the simulation testbench. These tools are effective for quickly identifying which portions of the HDL code that are not covered by functional test vectors. In general, the uncovered lines in the HDL code correspond either to redundant logic or uncovered functionality.

Code coverage tools on the one hand provide greater confidence in the overall verification methodology. On the other hand, code coverage tools do have certain limitations. For example, even if the testbench covers (execute during simulation) all lines of the HDL code, it does not necessarily mean that all functions in the specification are being tested. For instance, if a design has three required features and the RTL description captures only two of these features. It is possible that the testbench checks for only these two features and the code coverage tool might in turn ensure that every line of HDL code is in fact checked. However, the RTL can still be missing one of the required features. Thus, code coverage tools are not meant to ensure that the specifications are met. Instead they ensure that every line of HDL is in fact exercised during simulation. At the same time, it is also possible that the results of the HDL code that has been executed during simulation were never propagated through the design. This implies that HDL code that has been executed does not guarantee that the code has been tested.

3.3.2   Emerging Verification Coverage Methodologies

With increasing design sizes, verification has clearly become a serious bottleneck in the design process. Most importantly, developing test environments and the actual process of verification is often an extremely intensive manual effort. Besides, even the most comprehensive test plan is likely to miss certain functional bugs. Several different techniques are used to perform verification. Techniques such as the use of code coverage tools ensure that every line of the RTL description is exercised. On the other hand, cycle-based simulators help speed up the simulation run time. Another emerging area of verification tools focus on automating the verification process (self-checking tests) and providing metrics for the verification process as a whole [29]. Another technique involves the use of "assertion checkers" [30]. A third approach involves the use of a hardware verification language called Vera [27].

These new verification strategies have introduced a whole slew of verification "nomenclature" (or buzz words!) including: white-box testing, black-box testing, gray-box testing, glass-box testing etc. In general, a black box implies a lack of visibility into the internals of a module or design during the testing process. On the other hand, white box testing provides visibility to internal signals during the testing process. All other so-called "boxing" techniques involve different combinations of these two techniques and their definitions are often EDA vendor specific. This book does not discuss these emerging techniques in greater detail.

3.4 Simulator Interfaces

With increasing sizes of designs and the need to mix and match intellectual property (IP), a well-integrated simulation environment has become critical to the Verification methodology. Different parts of the design could potentially have different sources, constraints and environments. For example, an external IP might be in Verilog, while the design which requires this IP might be in VHDL. Another scenario, is when the design involves both analog and digital blocks. Under all of these scenarios, it is critical that the respective simulation environments "talk to each other". In this section, we discuss the different interfaces available to simulators, which enhance the value of the simulator by linking it with other simulators.

There are several kinds of simulator interfaces, applicable to various simulation scenarios. The Verilog language provides a standard Programmable Language Interface (PLI), which can be used to develop interfaces for Verilog-based simulators. VHDL-based simulators have proprietary interfaces. In this section, we cover the following simulator interfaces:

1. Foreign Language interface (C/C++).
2. Interface to hardware accelerators.

3. Interface to hardware/software models.

4. Mixed VHDL/Verilog simulators.

5. Mixed Analog/digital simulators.

6. SDF interface.

3.4.1 Foreign Language Interface

In several applications where the design contains mixed analog and digital components, the analog components can be best modeled using a high-level language like C or C++ (instead of Verilog or VHDL). To allow simulation of the design containing some (digital) modules written in Verilog/VHDL and other (analog) models written in C/C++, simulators provide an interface, known as foreign language interface for VHDL and Programming Language Interface (PLI) for Verilog.

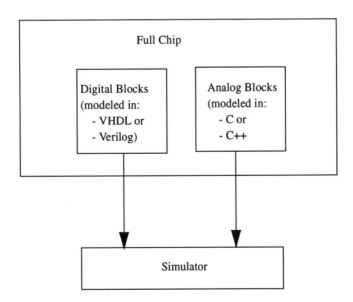

Figure 3.7 Foreign Language Interface

The architecture of the Foreign Language Interface for simulators is illustrated in Figure 3.7. For example, to co-simulate the C language models along with VHDL models (using a VHDL simulator), the following steps must be used:

1. Compile C models into a library and link them with the simulator to create a new simulator executable.

2. Create an entity-architecture template for the C models. This template will specify the ports in the C models and the names of C routines to execute whenever there is an event on the input ports. Example 3.1 shows the C-language interface (CLI) for Synopsys VSS simulator.

Example 3.1   Foreign Language Interface

```
entity ALU is
      Generic (DELAY: TIME := 4 ns);      -- output delay
      Port (command: in ALU_COMMANDS;
      strobe: in STD_LOGIC;
      data   : in STD_LOGIC_VECTOR;
      to     : out STD_LOGIC_VECTOR;
      status: out ALU_STATUS);
end ALU;


architecture CLI of ALU is
     attribute FOREIGN of CLI: architecture is "Synopsys:CLI";
     attribute CLI_ELABORATE of CLI: architecture is "Aleppine";
     attribute CLI_EVALUATE  of CLI: architecture is "alu_eval";
     attribute CLI_ERROR of CLI: architecture is "alu_error";
     attribute CLI_CLOSE of CLI: architecture is "alu_close";
     attribute CLI_PIN of command: signal is CLI_PASSIVE;
     attribute CLI_PIN of strobe: signal is CLI_ACTIVE;
     attribute CLI_PIN of data  : signal is CLI_PASSIVE;
       begin
       end;
```

Here "alu_open", "alu_eval", "alu_error", and "alu_close" are the names of C-routines that should be evaluated during initialization, change on active inputs, error, and completion of simulation respectively. This process is illustrated in Figure 3.8. "cli_active" causes the simulation to evaluate the component, whenever there is an event on the signal. On the other hand cli_passive does not cause the simulation to evaluate the component, when there is an event on a signal.

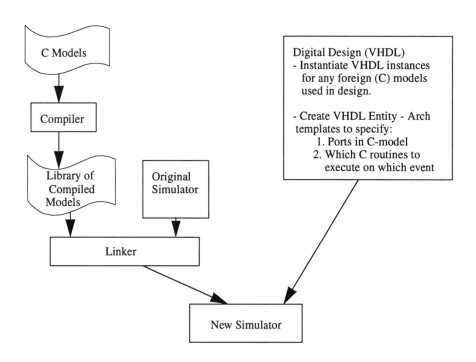

Figure 3.8 C interface to VHDL simulators.

3.4.2   Interface to Hardware Accelerators

Gate-level simulations are typically very compute intensive and time consuming. Hardware accelerators (e.g. IKOS) provide a mechanism to accelerate the simulation process by use of specialized hardware. Thus, a greater number of vectors can be used and hence help test the design to a greater extent. It is often desirable to use one simulation environment for the RTL and gate-level simulations. This is precisely what a simulator's interface to hardware accelerators provides. For example, it is possible to use the HDL simulator for RTL simulations and then use the HDL simulator interface to the hardware accelerator for faster gate-level simulations. The simulator's interface to hardware accelerator provides the same user interface and debug environment and helps seamlessly run simulations on the hardware accelerator as shown in Figure 3.9.

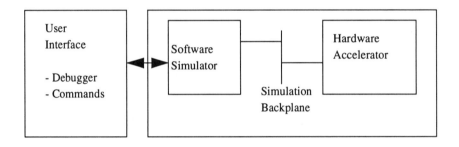

Figure 3.9 Interface to Hardware Accelerator.

3.4.3   Interface to Hardware/Software Models

Simulating a design as part of a larger system is critical to ensure the working of the entire system as shown in Figure 3.10. There are two ways to accomplish this, namely, using software models or hardware models.

1. Use of software (VHDL, Verilog) models to specify the system which drives the UUT. Commonly used software models can be obtained from EDA vendors. Software models can be instantiated in the design for simulation.

2. Use hardware model for the system driving the UUT. Commonly used models can be obtained from EDA vendors (e.g. Logic Modeling division of Synopsys). Hardware models provide significant speedup over similar software models.

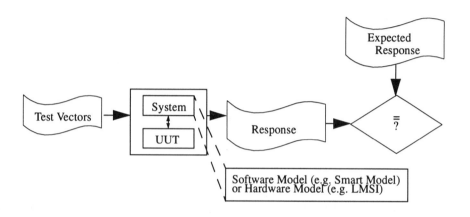

Figure 3.10   Modeling the system using a testbench.

3.4.4   Interface to Mixed VHDL/Verilog Simulation

The design community has standardized on two hardware description languages, namely, VHDL and Verilog. To share design knowledge (design cores) between VHDL and Verilog users, the simulator should be capable of simulating a design which instantiates both VHDL and Verilog blocks. This is possible using mixed VHDL/Verilog simulators.

Conventional simulators are designed for a single language (VHDL or Verilog). To allow mixed VHDL/Verilog simulation, two simulators (one VHDL and other Verilog) are hooked up together using a general purpose simulation backplane [26], which transfers events across the two simulators. This approach does have its limitations. When the design is heavily fragmented into VHDL and Verilog modules, then the backplane overhead can significantly slow down the simulation. Further, the two simulators are likely to have their own debug and simulation environments, making it difficult for the user to debug the design across language boundaries.

A second approach is to have unified simulation kernel (for example FusionHDL from Viewlogic) which uses optimized routines instead of a general purpose simulation backplane to transfer and synchronize events between two simulation engines running as a single process. This offers speedup over conventional simulation backplane approach. The unified kernel approach can be combined with a common user interface and debugging environment to provide a good solution for mixed VHDL-Verilog designs.

Another approach for mixed VHDL/Verilog simulation is known as unikernel simulation (e.g., Model Tech). The unikernel simulators use a single simulation engine for simulating designs containing mixed VHDL and Verilog modules. They also provide a single user interface and debug environment. These simulators are most efficient when multiple VHDL and Verilog models exist. They may however not be very efficient when the design is predominantly VHDL or predominantly Verilog, because compromises have to be made in the implementation of the engine to support the significant differences in the two languages.

3.4.5   Interface to Analog Simulators (mixed A/D simulation)

Mixed signal designs typically contain both analog and digital components. To simulate the complete design, the simulator should be capable of simulating both digital and analog components. Simulation backplane approach is used to address this problem, where events are transferred across analog simulator (e.g. Hspice) and digital simulator (e.g. Verilog XL).

The limitation with this approach is that typically the speed of digital simulators far exceeds the speed of analog simulators and the simulation run-time is determined by the analog simulator. If the existing analog simulator (for example Hspice) is not capable of simulating the complete analog block in a reasonable amount of time, then the purpose of mixed analog/digital simulator is defeated.

3.4.6 SDF Interface

The pre-route (estimated) and post-route cell and interconnect delays are used by the simulator for full-timing simulations (dynamic timing analysis). These delays are specified in a Standard Delay Format (SDF) file. The simulator can read in the delay values from the SDF file and annotate them on the simulation primitives. This is possible using the SDF interface for the simulator. The SDF writer and the code to be tested must follow consistent naming conventions (e.g. for hierarchical net and cell names) to effectively overlay the delay values for simulation.

VITAL Models: The VHDL Initiative Towards ASIC Libraries (VITAL) is an industry initiative to accelerate the availability of ASIC libraries across commercial VHDL simulators. The intent is to define a modeling specification that is compliant with IEEE standards such as 1076 and 1164, and utilizes the SDF timing format.

Prior to the use of VITAL models, the support for VHDL libraries from ASIC vendors was limited. Besides, the available libraries available were too slow for simulation purposes. In order to speed up simulation, the VHDL library used simulator-dependent primitives to achieve better performance. This meant the simulation methodology was tied to a specific commercial simulator. Further, for back annotation, the only standard way to annotate timing information was through the use of a "configuration" file, but this method was also too slow to compile. On the other hand Verilog users had an established means of annotating information using SDF.

Most present day VHDL simulators support VITAL models and hence its usage is gaining in acceptance. VITAL is intended to deliver the desired accuracy at an acceptable level of performance. EDA vendors are constantly improving simulation speeds using VITAL models. VITAL models ensure that VHDL users can stay in the VHDL environment in higher levels as well as when the design is in the gate level. This has its benefits because designers can use the same test bench for RTL verification as well as verification at the gate level. Further, the use of VITAL models will ensure that discrepancy between simulators will no longer be a cause for concern. Also, with the use of VITAL models, library developers can concentrate on one set of models that support VHDL simulators from a range of EDA vendors.

3.5 Conventional Simulation Methodology Limitations

In this section, we review the conventional simulation methodology and some of its limitations with respect to the emerging design and technology trends. A typical simulation flow consists of the following steps. Architectural level verification is done by specifying the design at a high level and simulating it using system simulators (like SPW, COSSAP) or VHDL/Verilog based simulators. The design is then partitioned into Analog and Digital blocks. Digital blocks are translated into RTL level description (synthesizable code) in VHDL/Verilog. Full-chip simulation at the RTL level is done by specifying analog blocks in C and using C-language interface of VHDL/Verilog based simulators. At this point, simulation verifies functionality but not timing. The RTL design is synthesized to obtain gate-level netlist. An SDF file containing estimated cell and net delays is also generated using a delay calculator. Full timing simulation is then done using event-driven simulators by back-annotating delays from the SDF file. Hardware accelerators are used to speed up simulation, because gate-level simulation takes a lot more time to run than RTL simulations.

Once the design is placed and routed, a new SDF file is generated containing accurate cell and net delays based on actual interconnect capacitances. Full timing simulation is done again with event-driven simulators with delays annotated from this new SDF file. Post-route simulation is also done using hardware accelerators to obtain acceptable performance. The same testbenches are used at all levels of simulation. The testbenches comprise of self-checking code. Testbenches may include hardware/software models to simulate the design as part of a larger system.

The increase in sizes of designs significantly impacts the verification methodology in general. In high density and high speed devices, for instance, accurately testing all timing paths in the design with conventional methods like simulation is a serious challenge. Simulation requires a very large number of test vectors for reasonable coverage of functionality. Thus, test vector generation is a significant effort. An increase in the number of test vectors implies, simulation run times that are extremely long. As simulation run-time starts becoming a bottleneck, designers are forced to resort to reducing the number of test vectors, which degrades the design quality due to reduced coverage. The following approaches have been used to progressively improve simulation run times by simulation tool vendors: Compiled code simulators instead of interpretive simulators, Native code simulators instead of general compiled code simulators, and the use of Hardware Accelerators and Emulators.

New techniques and tools that improve the verification methodology are constantly being developed and implemented. These include Cycle-based simulation, Formal Verification and Static Timing Analysis. Of these, Static Timing Analysis is widely used. Formal Verification and Cycle-based simulation tools are commercially available and beginning to be adopted by design houses. Static Timing Analysis is a technique that performs all timing checks such as setup, hold, recovery and removal times in a synchronous design without applying test vectors. Static timing analysis tools accomplish this by exhaustively tracing every possible timing path in the design, calculating delays on these paths, and reporting timing violations, if any. Chapter 5 discusses Static Timing methodology in greater detail while Formal Verification and Cycle based simulation are introduced in subsequent sections in this chapter.

3.6 Cycle-Based Simulation

Cycle-based simulation is a technique whereby an entire synchronous design is partitioned into series of storage elements and combinatorial functions. In cycle simulation there are no delays, every storage element is computed in every cycle, eliminating the need to schedule events and need to evaluate signals between cycle boundaries. Cycle-based simulation technology promises to offer verification speeds of 100 to 1000 cycles per second on large designs. In contrast, event driven simulators use complex algorithms to keep track of timing and may have to evaluate some functions multiple times in a single clock cycle.

Large systems, microprocessors, ASICs requiring very large number of simulation vectors to adequately validate their designs are primary applications for Cycle-based simulation. Cycle-based technology takes advantage of the fact that most electronic designs are synchronous. In synchronous designs the simulator needs to compute the steady state responses of a circuit at each clock cycle eliminating all scheduling overhead, leading to extremely fast simulations. Cycle-based simulators support the synthesizable subset of HDL. Thus, it is well suited to synthesizable designs.

Gate-level simulations, in general, are extremely time consuming. On the other hand, simulations and regression testing at the RTL level is far less time consuming. The need for cycle simulators is driven by the shift in verification methodology from dynamic timing simulation to a combination of fast function simulation and static timing analysis. The shift in methodology requires fast functional simulation at the RTL level and timing verification using static timing analysis tool at the gate level as shown in Figure 3.11. However, accurate high speed gate level simulation will continue to be an important part of the design cycle for the following reasons:

1. It is critical to ensure that the synthesized netlist is "equivalent" to the RTL description.

2. Most Design methodologies still require each portion of the circuit to undergo some degree of gate level timing simulation in the context of the rest of the chip. Many ASIC Vendor sign-off requirements include a full gate level timing simulation of the entire chip prior to vendor hand-off. Due to performance bottlenecks in event driven simulation this will be done with a very limited set of test vectors, and will be used primarily as a "plausibility" test of the gate level netlist.

The advantage of cycle based simulation over event driven simulation is that it is faster because unlike event driven simulators, cycle simulators have a predefined evaluation order, all functions are evaluated once, during the clock cycle. By not simulating timing data structures, circuit element computations are greatly simplified, resulting in a greater simulation performance, and reduced memory usage.

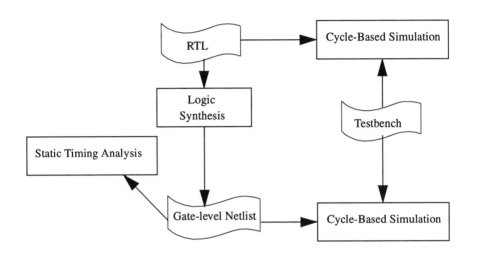

Figure 3.11 Cycle-Based Simulation Methodology.

For example, in the synchronous design in Figure 3.12, combinational logic blocks C1 and C2 are evaluated on clock edges, unlike an event driven simulator where C1 block is evaluated every time any of the inputs I1,I2, and I3 change. The disadvantage of a cycle simulation over event driven simulation is that it is not capable of identifying timing errors, such as setup and hold timing violations and glitches.

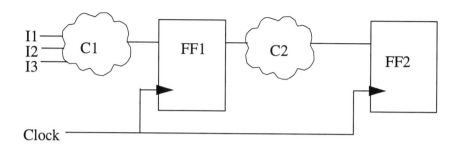

Figure 3.12 Registers with Intermediate Combinational Logic blocks

3.7 Formal Verification

Formal verification methodology has several applications. It can be used to verify a design against a reference design as it progresses through the different levels of abstractions as illustrated in Figure 3.13. For instance, after logic synthesis the RTL description can be compared to the gate-level netlist for equivalence. Similarly, after scan insertion the gate-level netlist prior to scan insertion can be compared to the netlist after scan insertion. Formal Verification tools have the capability to "turn-off" specific modules or instances in the design, or set signals to certain pre-defined values etc. while checking for equivalence. Thus, it is far from a "push-button" methodology, and involves significant setup and debugging. Though the figure indicates use of formal verification at every stage, this is far from the reality in present-day design flows. Besides, some *formal verification capabilities such as equivalence of Behavioral to RTL are not currently available.*

In short, formal verification is a powerful technology which is beginning to gain acceptance, and is likely to serve as a fundamental verification methodology for future designs. In general, Formal Verification does not require the use of any test vectors. Thus, formal Verification is analogous to Static Timing Analysis. Just as Static Timing Analysis verifies timing without vectors and Formal Verification verifies functionality without vectors.

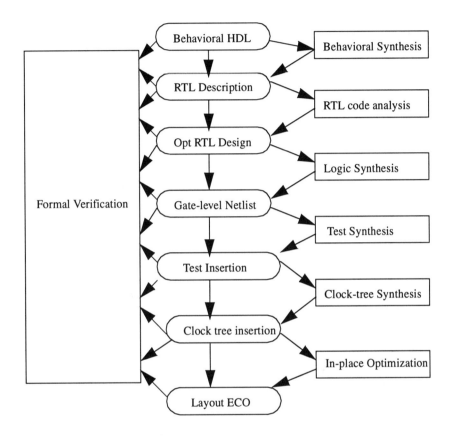

Figure 3.13 Potential Applications of Formal Verification

Formal Verification tools can be divided into three main categories, namely, Equivalence checking, Model Checking and Theorem provers.

Model Checkers compare a design to an existing set of logical properties of a design's behavior. These properties are a direct representation of the specifications of the design. The use of model checkers is more involved than equivalence checking. This is because the properties need to be generated by the user.

Theorem proving method of formal verification is the most advanced of the available formal verification techniques. It is far more involved than both equivalence checking and model checking and requires changes to the basic design flow. This approach requires that the design be represented using a "formal" specification language. Present-day hardware description languages such as VHDL and Verilog are unsuitable for this purpose, as they have no formal semantics. At each level of abstraction in the design flow, a theorem prover is used to ensure that the design corresponds to the original specification.

Equivalence checking is the most widely used of the three formal verification techniques. The other two techniques are still largely topics of research with a few commercial tools beginning to surface. Equivalence checking uses a mathematical approach to verify equivalence of a reference and a revised design. In this form of verification, the tool performs an exhaustive check on the two designs to ensure that the designs behave identically under all possible conditions.

Equivalence checking tools can be used to verify equivalence of different RTL or gate level implementations as illustrated in Figure 3.14.

One of the limitations of Formal Verification is that it assumes that the reference design is correct. If there are any errors in the reference design, they will not be detected in the revised design. Therefore, it is critical that the reference design is functionally correct. Another limitation of Formal Verification is that it does not verify timing. Therefore it must be used in conjunction with a Static Timing Analysis tool (e.g. Design Time, Veritime, Motive, PrimeTime etc.).

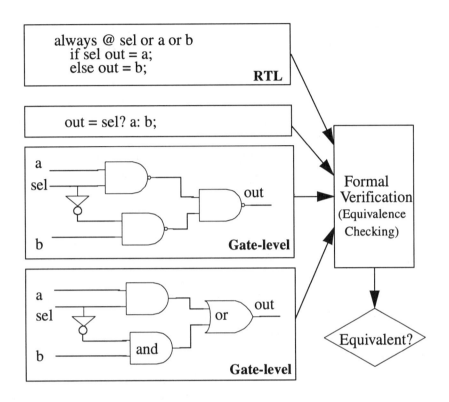

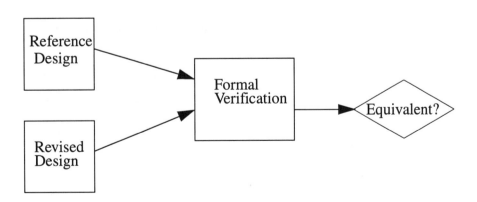

Figure 3.14 Equivalence Checking (Formal Verification)

3.8 Making the Transition

Traditionally, event-driven simulation have been used to verify both timing and functionality of a design. As a result of increasing design size, complexity, and time to market pressure, event driven simulators due to their long run times, are becoming a bottleneck for design verification. One alternative is to separate functional and timing verification. Timing verification can be accomplished independently using static timing analysis tools. Functional verification can be achieved using cycle-based simulation techniques. Further, formal verification provides a mechanism for verifying complete functional equivalence without test vectors, by mathematically proving functional equivalence between two different abstractions of the same design.

Making drastic changes in existing simulation methodology can introduce a lot of risks. Also, on the other hand, continuing with existing methodology for a long period of time would increase the risk of losing competitive edge and adversely impacting quality and time to market. A few key factors that are critical to progressing into the next generation of simulation/verification technology are as follows:

Introduce/Enhance the usage of Static Timing Analysis in the design flow: Full timing simulations at the gate-level is the most time consuming part of the simulation methodology. Static timing analysis is capable of complete timing verification without a vector set in a matter of hours as opposed to simulation which takes days or even weeks. The disadvantage lies in that static timing tools do not detect glitches.

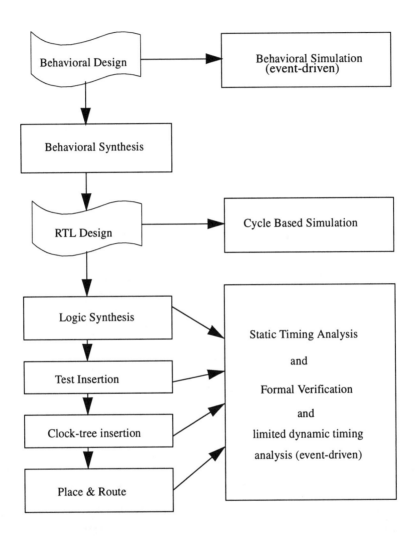

Figure 3.15 Future Verification Methodology.

Perform Unit Delay Simulations in conjunction with Static Timing Analysis: Once Static Timing Analysis methodology is established, use unit delay simulations instead of full timing simulation for different iterations of synthesis. Continue with full timing simulation as final checkoff simulation until enough confidence is developed with static timing analysis. Most ASIC vendors still insist on gate-level simulation for "sign-off".

Introduce Cycle-Based Simulation for RTL designs: If the design style is mostly synchronous, start using cycle-based simulation for RTL designs. Once static timing analysis methodology is implemented, full timing event-driven simulation can be gradually substituted. One can then rely on cycle-based and unit delay simulation for fast functional verification and static timing analysis for complete timing verification. A transition to this methodology is largely dependent on the continuing maturity of formal verification tools and the support of static timing analysis as a "sign-off" criteria for ASIC vendors in place of full timing simulation.

Use Formal verification to verifying functionality: Start using formal verification for verifying functionality as the design progresses through synthesis, test insertion, clock-tree insertion, place and route etc. The final methodology is illustrated in Figure 3.15.

In summary, simulation has been conventionally used for functional and timing verification of digital designs. Due to increasing design sizes and decreasing chip turnaround time requirements, simulation is becoming a bottleneck. Some advances have been made in the simulation technology to improve its performance, such as Compiled code simulators, Hardware accelerators, Cycle-based simulators and Hardware emulators. Static timing analysis (instead of simulation) is now increasingly being adopted for timing verification. Formal Verification technology is emerging for functional verification of designs. Transitioning to new methodologies using cycle-based simulation, static timing analysis, and formal verification should be done in phases to minimize the risks involved in adopting new technologies which have not yet been tested for the designs. The next generation simulation methodology would include, the use of cycle-based simulation for verifying RTL designs, static timing analysis to verify the timing of the gate-level design, (both pre-layout and post-layout) and formal verification to verify the functionality of the RTL design during RTL debug iterations and gate-level design after synthesis, test-insertion, clock-tree insertion and layout. In addition, tools such as code coverage tools, assertion checkers, verification based on hardware verification languages etc. will continue to be developed and deployed as part of the verification process.

3.9 Methodology Audit

This section covers certain basic queries relating to verification methodology in general. The intent is to serve as an "audit" that can help the reader identify potential areas of improvement for the verification methodology in general.

1. Have you considered the use of cycle-based simulation as means to perform fast functional verification, particularly, if your designs are mostly synchronous?

2. If you use VHDL as your language of choice, does your current simulation methodology involve the use of VITAL models?

3. Does your current methodology involve full-chip simulation? With increasing sizes of chips this can be a significant challenge especially with mixed signal designs. However, a full-chip simulation is critical to the overall verification of the design.

4. Have you considered Emulation as a means to perform fast prototyping and hardware/software co-simulation?

5. Is equivalence checking (formal verification) part of your current design flow?

6. Do you use code coverage tools used to ensure that all lines of the HDL code are exercised during simulation?

7. Do your designs involve integration of Intellectual Property (IP) blocks? If so, does the overall simulation testplan involve stimulating the IP block and verifying its responses in the context of the entire design?

8. Do you have any comparison data of Hspice simulation to actual gate-level simulation for your technology library? In other words, if you perform a timing simulation of a path with back-annotated loads in both Hspice and at the gate-level, what margin of error can you expect?

9. Is simulation run-time a serious issue for you? If so, have you explored verification methodologies such as Formal Verification, Cycle-based Simulation, Hardware Acceleration?

10. Are you aware of or have you considered using assertion checkers, spec-based verification, high-level verification language based verification and other new verification methodologies?

CHAPTER 4   *Logic Synthesis*

The transition to HDL based designs and logic synthesis has helped significantly increase the number of "gates per engineer per day" when compares to schematic capture based design. The nuances of the synthesis process significantly impact not only the final netlist generated, but also a broad spectrum of issues ranging from HDL coding styles and design partitioning, to CAD methodology in general. Hence, it is important to understand the fundamental concepts related to logic synthesis. What are the typical strategies involved in effectively optimizing a design using logic synthesis? This chapter addresses each of these issues in detail and is organized as follows. First we discuss optimization constraints and design rule constraints. This is followed by a discussion on basic logic synthesis concepts. The next section describes the synthesis environment and strategies for optimizing a design. Then, a sample design is described and all the synthesis concepts are illustrated. The last section introduces the concept of datapath synthesis and the overall flow involving logic synthesis.

4.1 Introduction

Logic Synthesis is the process of converting a design description written in a hardware description language like Verilog or VHDL into gates from the technology library, based on user-specified optimization constraints. This synthesizable HDL code is referred to as Register Transfer Level code. This coding style is one in which the cycle to cycle behavior of the design is described in the HDL code. The process of converting an HDL description to gates involves two steps, namely, translation and optimization. After translating an HDL description to gates, optimization of the gates is performed based on user-specified constraints to generate an optimal netlist. Commercial logic synthesis tools typically support Timing, Area and Power optimization constraints. Some of the features of logic synthesis include register inferencing, resource sharing, implementation selection, ease of re-targeting to a new process technology, constraint-driven optimization etc. Effective logic synthesis strategies and accurate modeling of timing constraints for synthesis are imperative for an optimal design.

This chapter discusses logic synthesis concepts in general. However, most concepts and terminologies are tailored to the Design Compiler tool from Synopsys Inc., the leading logic synthesis tool in the market. Other commercial alternatives such as BuildGates from Ambit Design Systems, Inc. are also available. Both Design Compiler and BuildGates are meant for standard cell designs. FPGA designs require the use of FPGA synthesis tools. Appendix A lists a few of the different commercial standard cell and FPGA synthesis tools.

4.2 Logic Synthesis Based ASIC Design Flow

The design flow begins with an HDL description, a set of design constraints and the desired technology library being provided to a synthesis tool such as Synopsys Design Compiler. The HDL description is then synthesized to a technology specific netlist that meets the design constraints specified. At this juncture, the design is ready for test synthesis. The first step in the test synthesis process is to execute test design rule checking to ensure that there are no test violations in the design. This is followed by scan insertion after fixing any violations that might be identified in the previous step. Test synthesis tools also provide the capability to perform stitching of scan chains in addition to scan insertion. The entire test synthesis process is described in greater detail in chapter 6.

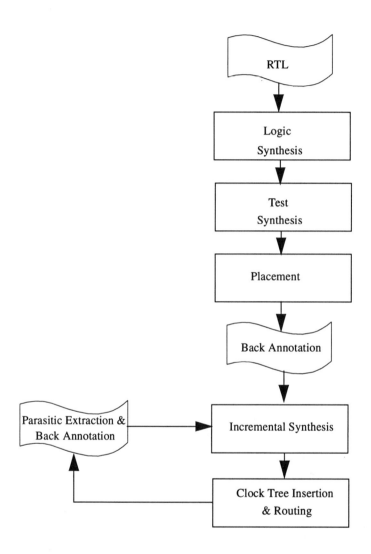

Figure 4.1 High Level Logic Synthesis Flow

Figure 4.1 shows the logic synthesis design flow while Figure 4.2 shows the same flow with greater level of detail. Both figures assume the need for testability and hence shows the steps involved in scan insertion. The Verification steps are however not shown in the figure

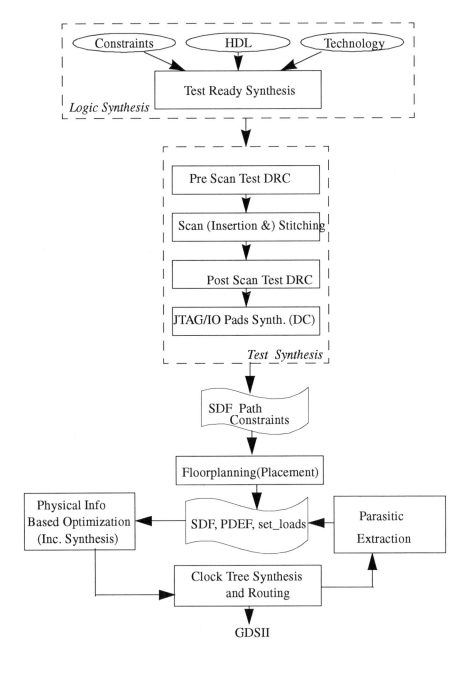

Figure 4.2 Detailed Logic Synthesis Flow

since the intent is to concentrate on only the logic synthesis aspects of the flow. It is assumed that design verification is performed at different levels of abstraction in the design flow such as RTL and gate-level.

Following test synthesis (i.e., scan insertion), is the test design rule checking step. This step is identical to the pre-scan design rule checking except for the fact that the design now has scan inserted. At this stage, the design is ready for floor-planning and placement. Following which, back annotation of capacitive load is performed on the design and it is re-synthesized to meet the new timing constraints based on delay information generated after placement (custom wire load models can be generated as discussed in chapter 1). The netlist is then routed and extraction of parasitics is performed. At this stage, the true parasitics based on actual routing is available. This information is back-annotated to check for any timing violations that might exist. After fixing of timing problems a new netlist is generated which is then incrementally placed and routed through an Engineering Change Order (ECO) flow.

4.3 Constraints for Logic Synthesis

Logic Synthesis tools convert HDL code to gates based on user-specified Optimization constraints and Design rule constraints imposed by the technology library. Timing, area and power are the three optimization constraints provided to the logic synthesis tool. While commercial logic synthesis for timing and area have been in use for several years, optimization for power is a relatively new development. This requires that the logic synthesis technology library include details on cell power dissipation. Similarly, max capacitance, max transition time and max fanout are the three design rule constraints. In this section, we describe each of these constraints in greater detail.

4.3.1 Optimization Constraints

One of the objectives of logic synthesis is to meet the optimization constraints specified by the user. Optimization constraints include timing, area and power constraints.

Timing Constraints: When optimizing a design to meet timing constraints, the synthesis tool aims to meet setup and hold constraints on the sequential elements in the design. Setup constraint for an edge triggered sequential element is defined as the time interval before the active clock edge during which the data should remain unchanged. Hold constraints on the other hand, are defined as the time interval after the active clock edge during which the data should remain unchanged. Specifying timing constraints involves identifying the clock periods and waveforms for the different clocks in the design (both external clocks and any internally generated clocks). In addition, for each of the clocks, information such as clock tree delay and maximum clock skew on the die are also to be provided. During synthesis this information may not be accurately available. Hence, it is important that estimates be specified based on inputs from the ASIC vendor and information about the number of registers driven by each clock source. The intent is to provide the synthesis tool estimated values so that enough margin is built into the design during the synthesis process.

All synchronous paths are completely constrained by specifying the clock periods and waveforms for all the clock sources. For asynchronous paths, timing constraints need to be provided. For example, the `set_max_delay` command is used to constrain asynchronous paths in the Design Compiler to the maximum delay allowed. Further, timing information about the design environment must be provided for all the ports of the design. The time at which data becomes valid on the input ports and the clock domains with which they are referenced needs to be provided. In Design Compiler, this is achieved using the `set_input_delay` commands. Similarly for all the output ports, the timing requirements must be specified. These constraints are based on the logic driven by the output ports and the clock domain of the destination register. In DC, the `set_output_delay` command is used to provide this information (as discussed in section 4.4).

Area Constraints: Area constraints specify the maximum area for the design. Timing constraints have the highest priority among the different optimization constraints. Hence, if both timing and area constraints are provided, the tool reduces area after meeting timing constraints. In other words, area improvements are made only if they do not violate timing constraints.

Power Constraints: There are several aspects to power optimization. Firstly, low power design begins with a "global" focus on reducing power. This means, considering power reduction at every stage, as the design traverses through different levels of abstraction in the flow. For example, at the system level, different parts of the system might operate at different voltages. By careful partitioning and the effective use of the power down mode, power reduction can be achieved at the system level.

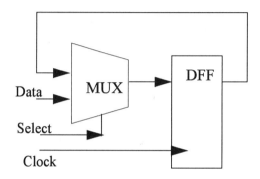

Flip-flop continuously enabled

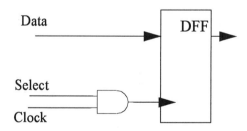

Flip-flop active only when enabled

Figure 4.3 Use of Gated Clocks

At the algorithmic level of abstraction, complexity and concurrency have a direct impact on the power consumption. Similarly, at the architectural level, parallelism and pipelining impact the power consumption. At the back-end of the design flow, power reduction is possible through reduced interconnects and transistor sizing. For example, standard cell libraries in general are more power efficient than similar gate array libraries due to the use of varying transistor sizes and optimized layouts.

Logic synthesis for power, however, concentrates on optimization at the logic level. This means that it is possible to significantly reduce power consumption in a design by following certain design styles and using appropriate low power cells from the technology library. Power based synthesis algorithms are dependent on the toggle information provided for all the inputs and bi-directional ports. This information is derived from functional HDL simulation. Thus, one approach to reducing power is to minimize operations and signal transitions that do not affect the functionality of the design. This means, parts of the design must be "turned off" when not required. "Gated Clocks" is one technique to achieve this. A typical application is when there is feedback from the output of a register that is multiplexed with the input data as shown in Figure 4.3. In this design, the flip-flop is in constant use irrespective of any change in input data. In such situations, it is possible to reduce power by inserting a gated clock. Adding a gate before the clock pin, ensures that the flip-flop is active (or operational) only when the select line is active. When using a bank of registers this technique can significantly reduce power consumption. However, the use of gated clocks does involve some trade-offs. Firstly, use of gated clocks makes timing verification complicated due to the use of a control signal. Further, it impacts testability, clock tree synthesis, skew balancing and can cause glitches. There are several additional techniques to reduce power in designs. Further discussion on these techniques is beyond the scope of this book.

4.3.2   Design Rule Constraints

The constraints imposed on the geometry of an integrated circuit layout, in order to guarantee fabrication with an acceptable yield are called design rules [1]. In other words, Design Rule constraints ensure that the layout of the design is feasible. In general, design rules are process technology specific. The design rules imposed during the synthesis phase are different from those in the physical domain. In this section, we discuss the design rules imposed during logic synthesis. "Max Transition", "Max Capacitance" and "Max Fanout" are the commonly used design rules.

Max Transition: Transition time is defined as the time required for a net to change logic values. Typically, it is measured as the time to change from 10% to 90%, though it could be measured differently. The max transition time constraint, usually imposed by the technology, is the maximum transition time for nets in the design. This constraint is met during synthesis by using higher drive cells and by appropriately buffering to drive high loads. Typically, after the placement of design, the net capacitances are estimated and based on which any transition time violations are fixed in an incremental synthesis step. This stage in the synthesis process involves up-sizing or down-sizing of cells or the addition of buffers.

Max Capacitance: This constraint determines the maximum capacitive loading allowed on a certain cell. This constraint is typically different for each cell in the library. The intent is to provide the synthesis tool a series of alternatives from which the tool can select the most appropriate cell based on the timing and area constraints. However, it is also possible to specify a global value for all cells in the technology library.

Max Fanout: This constraint is used for modeling the loading of the primitive cells in the library. It specifies the fanout a particular cell can have in the design without violating design rule constraints. For example, a max fanout of 5 in Synopsys DC, implies that the cell can drive upto 5 fanout loads. The inputs pins of all cells in the Synopsys library have `fanout_load` values specified. The sum of the fanout load values on all the input pins must not exceed the max fanout of the drive cell output pin.

4.4 Describing the Synthesis Environment

In this section, we discuss the information required to describe the synthesis environment and how that information is used during synthesis. The concepts discussed are in general applicable to any logic synthesis tool. Figure 4.4 describes a sample design in a given design environment.

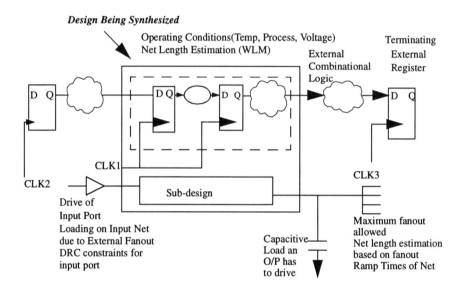

Figure 4.4   A Sample Design and its Environment

With the scenario in Figure 4.4 in mind we present the design environment and a mechanism for describing the same for a logic synthesis tool. Figure 4.5 shows the different constraints to be specified in Synopsys Design Compiler and Example 4.1 shows the corresponding dc_shell script.

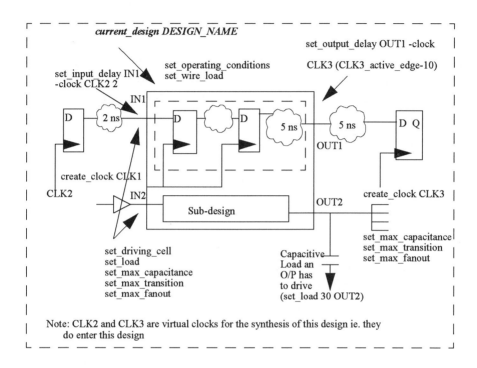

Figure 4.5 Design environment described for Synopsys DC

Example 4.1   Synopsys dc_shell script

```
current_design my_design
create_clock -period 10 CLK1
create_clock -period 10 -name CLK2
create_clock -period 10 -name CLK3
set_input_delay 2 IN1 -clock CLK2
set_wire_load my_wire -lib my_lib
set_operating_conditions worst_case -lib my_lib
set_driving_cell -cell my_lib/FD1 all_inputs()
set_load 30 OUT2
set_max_transition 2.5 my_design
set_max_capacitance 2.5 my_design
set_max_fanout 2.5 my_design
```

Input Drive Strengths: This information is determined by the technology cell that drives a particular input port e.g., the NANDA cell or BUFD cell from a technology library. Based on the drive strength specified, the synthesis tool knows what kind of loads the input net can drive without violating any design rule constraints. Also, this information is used in calculating the transition time of the input nets.

Output Load: The capacitive loading of an output port and the number of cells it fans out to are used during synthesis to identify a cell with the appropriate drive strength to drive the output loads. During this process, the logic synthesis tool also ensures that the design rule constraints are not violated.

Input Arrival Time: For a synthesis tool to optimize a timing path in order to meet setup constraints, it is required to know the arrival times for the input ports. Further, it is required to identify the clock domain with respect to which the input signal is referenced. This information is used by the synthesis tool to determine the late arriving input signals and optimize paths accordingly.

Output Timing: In order to optimize timing paths leading to output ports, synthesis needs information on the external combinational delay and clock information of the terminating external register. Based on this information, the tool derives the timing constraints for paths terminating at output ports. This information tells the synthesis tool how much time of a clock cycle is allocated within the block and to logic external to the block.

Wire-Load Model: The technology library is provided with wire load models to determine the net delays in a design. However, these wire load models are based on statistics of fanout and loads from several designs. Moreover, these wire-load models assume an aspect ratio of 1. This means it assumes that all logic blocks in the design are square shaped when generating the wire load model. For a certain fanout of a net and a certain design size, the wire load model provides the net length, net area, net capacitance and net resistance.

Example 4.2   Wire Load Model in Synopsys Library

```
wireload ("my_wire_load") {
```

```
capacitance = 0.5
resistance = 1.0
area = 0.0
slope : .83;
fanout_load (1, 0.25)
fanout_load (2, 0.50)
fanout_load (3, 0.75)
}
```

Example 4.2 shows the description of a wire load model in the Synopsys technology library. The values against resistance, capacitance and area are all defined in "per unit length". In other words, for example, the capacitance per unit length is 0.5 and the resistance per unit is 1.0. A value of 0 against the area implies that this wire load model does not account for wire area. The fanout_load defines the length for a particular fanout. For example, a fanout of 1 implies a wire length of 0.25. Thus, for a fanout of 1, the resistance would be the product of the resistance per unit length and the wire length (1 x 0.25 = 0.25 in this case). For fan-outs greater than 3, the slope value is used to extrapolate the wire length. In general, statistical wire-load models in a technology library are not very accurate. Further, this inaccuracy is more prominent in smaller geometries. To eliminate some of these inaccuracies custom wire-load models (as discussed in chapter 1) are created for a design after the first iteration of floor-planning and placement. Wire load models can be explicitly specified by the user, applied due to default wire loads specified in the technology library or automatically applied by the synthesis tools based on the size of a design or sub-design.

Operating Conditions: This information is used during synthesis to scale up or scale down delay numbers based on variation in temperature, voltage or process technology from the nominal values. This mechanism helps in modeling timing during synthesis for different process data points.

Example 4.3   Operating Conditions in the Synopsys Library Format

```
library (example) {
```

```
operating_conditions (WCCOM) {
    process : 0.35;
    temperature : 85;
    voltage : 3.3;
    tree_type : worst_case_tree;
  }
  }
```

In the Synopsys ".lib" template shown in Example 4.3, WCCOM identifies the set of operating conditions. The process scaling factor accounts for variations in the out-come of the actual semiconductor manufacturing steps, typically 1.0 for normal operating conditions. The temperature corresponds to the ambient temperature in which the design is to operate. Similarly, the voltage accounts for the operating voltage of the design. The "tree_type" refers to the interconnect model that is to be used by the synthesis tool in order to calculate delays. Other possible interconnect models include best_case_tree, worst_case_tree, and balanced_tree. Just as in the case of wire-load models, the operating_conditions group can be specified explicitly by the user, the default_operating_conditions specified in the library or the nominal operating conditions defined in the library group.

4.5 Logic Synthesis Concepts

In this section, we discuss some of the common logic synthesis capabilities and how they affect synthesis results.

4.5.1 Resource Sharing

Sharing the same hardware resource for mutually exclusive arithmetic operations is called resource sharing. In general, only arithmetic operations can be resource shared and not boolean operations. Moreover, arithmetic operations often translate into large hardware resources and hence imply a significant saving in area when shared unlike boolean operations which are relatively much smaller in area. HDL constructs like *if* and *case* statements imply mutual exclusivity.

Example 4.4   HDL example where the "addition" resource can be shared.

```
If (condition) then
    A <= B + C;
Else
    A <= D + E;
End if;
```

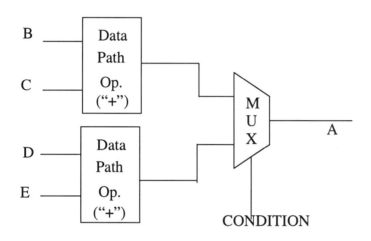

Figure 4.6 Design prior to resource sharing

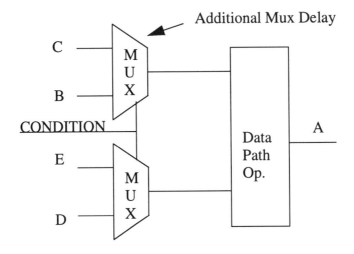

Figure 4.7 Resource Sharing

Note that resource sharing causes an additional delay due to the multiplexor. In general, resource sharing helps improve area at the expenses of timing. Thus, based on timing and area constraints resource sharing techniques are used by logic synthesis. Figure 4.6 shows a design where resource sharing can be applied. Note that in Figure 4.6 there are two datapath operators while in Figure 4.7 one datapath operator is shared to realize the same functionality.

4.5.2   Register Inference

Logic synthesis infers sequential elements in the design based on the HDL code as shown in Example 4.5. This means that based on the HDL function described and the sequential cells available in the technology library, logic synthesis selects the optimal cells for implementation e.g. D flip-flop, JK flip-flop, T flip-flop etc. Further, logic synthesis tools are also capable of inferring register banks. Recent advances in logic synthesis to incorporate test synthesis up-front (one-pass synthesis) have also made possible direct mapping to scan flip-flops during initial synthesis.

Example 4.5   Register Inference

```
--Verilog
always @ (posedge clock)
Q<= Data;

--VHDL
process
begin
  wait until clock' event and clock = '1';
  Q<= Data;
end process;
```

4.5.3   Implementation Selection

Selecting the appropriate implementation of an arithmetic operation to meet timing and area constraints is called implementation selection. For example, the "add" arithmetic operation has different possible architectures e.g. Ripple carry, carry-look ahead, carry look forward for an adder. These architectures have different timing and area characteristics for different bit-widths. Manually selecting the architecture based on the path timing constraints is not feasible. Logic synthesis addresses this problem by automatically performing implementation selection. For instance, the Synopsys Design Compiler synthesizes different possible architectures and stores them in a cache in the users home directory. Then, based on the required timing and area requirements, the Design Compiler uses the most appropriate implementation. It is possible to direct the synthesis tool to map to desired implementations through the use of tool-specific commands. This mechanism is made possible through the Synopsys DesignWare libraries. These libraries contain several technology-independent, testable, parametrizable and synthesizable components (or macro blocks) which can either be inferred from RTL during synthesis or directly instantiated in the source HDL.

4.6 Optimization Strategies

The methodology used to synthesize ASICs is very critical to the timely and successful implementation of the design. There are different strategies that can be used for synthesis. In this section, we will discuss the different approaches and the combinations of these that can be used to achieve successful synthesis. There are three basic synthesis strategies, namely, Hierarchical Compile, Time Budgeting and the Compile-characterize-write_script approach. Most synthesis strategies are usually a combination of one or more of these three basic strategies. New tools and methodologies that are capable of *automatic time budgeting* are commercially available and likely to gain in acceptance in the future.

4.6.1 Hierarchical Compile

This is the simplest approach and as the name implies consists of synthesizing the complete design after specifying all the timing information and constraints at the top level. This technique is also known as top-down compile and involves automatic time budgeting. In other words, the tool calculates all the different timing requirements in the design from the top level constraints provided by the user. This technique is very dependent on the memory of the machine as well as the CPU. However, there is a certain size (usually over 100-150K gates) beyond which the quality of results gets affected in this approach and run times become extremely large. As a very rough rule of thumb, designs over 100K gates should be broken into smaller blocks for synthesis. Designs that are datapath intensive, design with several path exceptions (functional false paths and multi-cycle paths) etc. are usually not suited to this compile strategy.

4.6.2 Time Budgeting

This is the most time consuming approach and requires a sound understanding of the design. In this approach, the designer decides the granularity (number of sub-blocks) at which synthesis is to be performed and develops time budgets for each of these blocks. These time budgets are approximate but the more accurate the approximation, the faster one can converge to the desired timing. Timing Budgets include information such as input signal arrival times, input signal drives, output signal timing requirements, output signal loads, clock sources and their clock tree characteristics, path exception information (functional false paths and multi-cycle paths) and any other relevant environment information. After synthesizing the individual blocks using specific time budgets, these blocks are then integrated and static timing analysis is performed to get information about critical timing paths, especially those that cross module boundaries. Then, based on the feedback from static timing analysis either a top level synthesis approach is used to address any constraint violations or the original time budget files are refined for a better first pass synthesis. Alternately, an incremental synthesis is performed to fix the timing violations.

Example 4.6   Time Budgeting

Consider a design example with three sub-designs "A", "B" and "C" at the top level. A, B and C are hierarchical sub-designs contained in "TOP". For synthesis, we optimize A, B and C independently rather than synthesize TOP. This implies that we need to create time budget files for each of these designs. Figure 4.8 shows the partitioning with three sub-designs A, B and C.

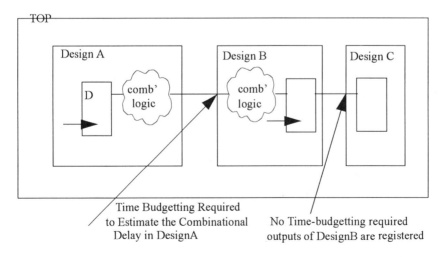

Figure 4.8 Design Partitioning

The first partition between A and B sub-designs has combinational outputs and hence requires accurate time budgeting. In other words, it is required to identify the approximate timing delays and drive strengths of inputs. In the second partition between B and C, the designs have been partitioned such that all outputs are registered. In this case, it is very easy to approximate the input timing delay numbers and drive requirements for design C as well as the output timing delay requirements for design B. Thus, time budgeting becomes relatively less complicated provided outputs of designs are registered.

4.6.3   Compile—Characterize—Write Script Approach

The manual time budgeting approach is very time consuming and at the same time requires good approximations in order to produce acceptable results. The hierarchical approach on the other hand is more brute force. As a result, a third approach was devised, that was more "middle of the road". In this approach, the top level timing specifications for the design are first identified. This task is relatively straightforward, since they are derived directly from the board level or overall specifications of the ASIC being designed. Then, all the sub-designs are synthesized initially with basic timing constraints. These blocks are then integrated together at the top level and top level timing constraints are applied.

"Characterize" is the Synopsys terminology for propagating timing and other environment information from the TOP (where TOP refers to the highest level of the design hierarchy of the ASIC) to specific sub-designs in the context of its existing ASIC environment. Without this capability, this would have to be done manually by the user. The next step in this flow is to characterize each of the sub-designs in the context of the top level timing specifications as well as the other sub-designs with which it interacts. Then, these sub-designs are synthesized using the characterized constraints. The characterize flow requires that the sub-designs first be synthesized to gates prior to execution of the characterize step. This means that if the initial constraints applied to the sub-blocks are inaccurate, this could impact the results of characterize. In such cases, meeting the desired timing constraints might take a few iterations. However, the biggest advantage to this approach, is that it is simple and can handle large designs. Besides, this approach lends itself to automation using "make" files.

However, with improvements in synthesis tools, the size of designs that tools can accept is increasing, thereby favoring a hierarchical compile approach over other techniques.

4.7 The Logic Synthesis—Floorplanning Link

Statistical wire load models are used during the initial phase of synthesis to estimate net loads and timing as discussed in section 4.4. Inaccurate wire load models significantly impact the convergence to a working netlist, particularly, for DSM designs. One way to address this is by creating custom wire-load models for the design (as discussed in chapter 1). In this approach, after floorplanning and placement, the net loads are estimated in the physical domain based on the placement and orientation of the blocks and the physical clusters created. These estimated loads are much more accurate than the wire-load models since they are generated based on the design rather than a statistical average. These wire loads can then be used to perform another iteration of synthesis. In general, back-annotation information from the Floor-planner/Placement tools to the Logic Synthesis domain include: Net loads, estimated Net and Cell Delays in Standard Delay Format (SDF), Net Resistances and Physical Cluster and Location Information via Physical Data Exchange Format (PDEF).

Optimization is often required to fix Setup Violations, Design Rule Violations and Hold Violations identified using back-annotation information. At this stage, the design has already been floor-planned and placed. Hence, re-synthesis of the design (unless the timing violations are too drastic) must be avoided in order to avoid new cell instance and net names. However, in a hierarchical placement and route flow, individual sub-blocks can be re-synthesized and placed and routed independently. Alternately, if physical clusters have been created during placement, the cells within the physical cluster can be re-synthesized after back-annotating the PDEF.

In short, after placement, the degree of flexibility is far more than after routing. In general, only up sizing and down sizing of cells, and buffering is allowed after routing. The changes made in the logic synthesis domain in each of the iterations can be conveyed back to the physical domain via an incremental PDEF and a new netlist. In general, synthesis using information from the physical domain has certain limitations since the logic synthesis tools do not take into account physical domain characteristics such as congestion, hard macro blockages etc.

4.7.1 Fixing Violations

Post-placement Setup Violations: Typically these violations are due to long nets. The violations can be fixed by re-synthesis of the critical paths, proper cell sizing and buffering of cells based on information from the physical domain.

Post-placement Design Rule Violations: In general, these are transition time violations or max capacitance violations caused by the inaccuracy of the net load estimates. Once again, this inaccuracy is a result of using statistical wire load models. These violations are fixed by appropriate cell sizing and buffering.

Post-Floorplanning Hold Violations: In the best case operating conditions, the hold violations are exaggerated. Hence, these violations are best analyzed in these conditions. In general, worst case operating conditions imply a condition where the delays are maximum. Similarly, best case operating conditions imply a condition data point where the

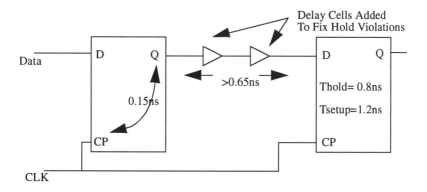

Figure 4.9 Fixing Hold Violations by Inserting Delays

delays are the minimum. Hold violations are fixed by adding delay cells to short timing paths in the design as shown in Figure 4.9. In the physical domain, they can be fixed by manually changing the placement of the cells so that the net delay increases to offset the hold violation. When placing delay cells in the physical domain in order to meet hold violations, they are often placed across the die since they are meant to delay the signals.

4.8 Technology Translation

One of the biggest advantages of logic synthesis is the ability to re-target a design description in RTL from one technology library to another. With support for synthesis libraries from potentially all ASIC vendors, logic synthesis has become a fundamental component of the ASIC design flow. However, prior to re-targeting a design from one technology to another, it often helps to have a "quick and dirty" estimate of the new target technology library with regard to availability of identical cells, performance etc. Technology translation is useful because, re-targeting to another library implies having to go through the entire design flow starting with the logic synthesis.

Porting a design involves converting the design from one technology to another. Automatic translation of a design netlist from one technology to another is supported by Design Compiler from Synopsys. Technology translation tries to map cells in the design from the current technology library to corresponding functionally equivalent cells from the new technology. When such a cell is not found, then it is built using other primitive discrete cells.

Typically, re-synthesis of the design is required after translation because translation considers only functional equivalence and does not consider timing. In other words, translating a design from one technology to another does not imply that the timing requirements of the design will be met. Hence, rather than translating the design fro one technology to another, designers often choose to re-synthesize the design (to the new target technology) beginning with the source RTL description. It might be required to modify the synthesis scripts to suit the capabilities of the new target technology.

4.9   Synthesis Case Study

In this section, we develop and discuss the synthesis strategy for an example ASIC. First, the hierarchy of the ASIC, its design characteristics and the technology library information are discussed. Then, an example methodology to synthesize the ASIC and specific reasons for the strategies used are outlined. Note that the intent is not to discuss all possible optimization strategies, but to suggest one possible approach. Design Compiler from Synopsys is the synthesis tool used, though the concepts are applicable to other commercial synthesis tools.

4.9.1   Case Study

This section describes a sample ASIC design and the issues related to the technology library that is to be used to synthesize the design. The intent is to discuss a typical ASIC with memories, standard cells, IP blocks, JTAG, I/O pads etc. The logical hierarchy of the ASIC is shown in Figure 4.10.

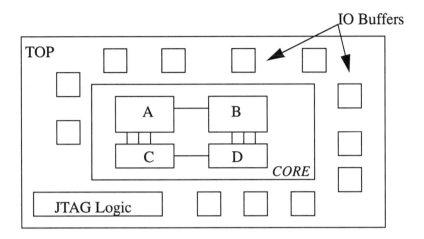

Figure 4.10 Design Hierarchy

1. The ASIC to be synthesized has over 250K gates and has three clock pins.

2. The logic synthesis library in use does not support automatic pad synthesis.

3. The JTAG components are being re-used from a previous ASIC. It is to be instantiated and connected at the top level of the design.

4. The synthesis technology library has two operating conditions defined, namely, "WCCOM" and "BCCOM". The former meets the requirements for the worst case while the latter for the best case conditions of the chip.

5. There are more than 10 statistical wire-load models described in the technology library, which also supports automatic wire load selection.

6. The ASIC synthesis library is modeled for transition time design rule constraints.

7. For test synthesis, the library supports the "multiplexed flip-flop" scan style and the "clocked scan" scan style. The design is expected to have full-scan rather than partial scan.

4.9.2   Analysis of The Case Study

Timing Constraints: At the outset, the top level ASIC timing specifications must be generated for synthesis. This consists of converting the chip timing and system board specifications to synthesis tool commands. The ASIC environment information (as shown in the example discussed in Figure 4.5) must include port capacitive loading, clock source timing data, timing waveforms of input and output ports etc.

Design Hierarchy: At the "TOP" level of the ASIC, the IO Buffers and JTAG logic and the design core are instantiated in the RTL code. Logic synthesis is performed at the "CORE" level. The core consists of several hierarchical blocks or sub-designs and synthesis is performed on each of these sub-designs. The core is formed by integrating these sub-designs and no optimization is performed at the core level. In general, it is not advisable to have any "glue" logic at the top level since it causes large compile run-times. Thus, any additional gates that need to be added to meet any timing requirements are to be done at the sub-design level rather than at the core level.

Sub-design Constraints: The next step is to derive the ASIC timing specifications at the "CORE" level. This can be automatically derived using the "characterize" command in Synopsys Design Compiler after specifying constraints at the top level of the design. However, it is required that the sub-designs be synthesized to gates using a preliminary set of constraints before the characterize technique can be used. At this stage it is important to specify the false paths and multi-cycle paths so that the initial synthesis of the sub-blocks is fairly accurate. The initial synthesis phase aims to fix all setup constraints in the design. Hence, the worst case operation conditions "WCCOM" must be used at this stage since the delays are maximum in this case. In order to fix hold constraints it is required to re-optimize (using in-place optimization or incremental compile) the design using the best case operating conditions "BCCOM".

Clocks: The clock tree can be generated by instantiating clock drivers in the HDL. Then, during the synthesis phase the clock network is "dont touched" to avoid adding or removing logic to or from the clock fanout. This is achieved using the `set_dont_touch_network` command in

Synopsys Design Compiler. Further, the estimated clock tree delay and skew numbers must be specified during synthesis. These numbers are usually estimated based on the number of loads on a clock domain. In Synopsys Design Compiler the clock tree timing information is specified using the `set_clock_skew -delay -uncertainty` command. Alternately, clock tree synthesis tools can be used to implement an optimal clock tree.

Test Synthesis: Inserting scan cells in a design is a part of the test synthesis process. However, it is possible to account for the impact of the scan cells up-front during logic synthesis. In other words, the one-pass synthesis capability can be used. This capability helps replace all sequential cells in the design with scan cells during initial synthesis. However, the actual stitching of the scan chain happens at a later stage. This prevents the need for incremental synthesis after test insertion in order to fix timing violations caused by additional delays due to scan cells.

Spare Cells: To allow Engineering Change Order (ECO) functional changes in the design after placement and routing, spare cells are instantiated in the RTL of the design. The spare cells can be ASIC vendor hard macros or discrete blocks of logic (soft macros) that are instantiated in the design. Typically each spare cell hard macro consists of several sequential elements and combinational logic gates. ASIC vendors usually provide a soft macro model for the spare cells, so that primitive cells from it might be utilized at the post-placement phase in order to fix any timing and functional problems. Spare cells are also used by physical domain tools to fix hold violations and DRC violations. Figure 4.11 shows the detailed logical hierarchy of the ASIC.

4.9.3   The Synthesis Steps

Figure 4.11 shows the design hierarchy in detail with sub-design names and instance names, gate counts, external IP blocks, memories, JTAG logic and I/O pads. Listed below are few characteristics that influence the synthesis steps.

1. Design C has critical timing paths and several functional false paths.

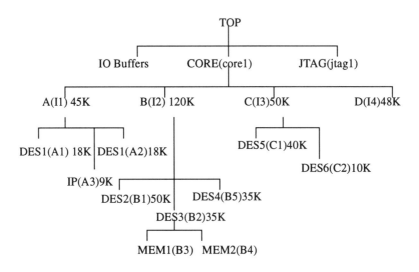

Figure 4.11 Detailed Design Hierarchy

2. Design A includes an external IP block which is available as a fully synthesized standard cell netlist.

3. Des3 has two memory blocks MEM1 and MEM2, both of which are RAM BIST and hard macro RAMs.

4. Designs D and A have acceptable compile times when compiled hierarchically.

To start with, the RTL code for the designs must be analyzed and elaborated. At this stage a technology independent format of the design is saved. During this process, incorrect latch inference and incomplete sensitivity lists can be identified. During synthesis, instantiate the hard macro memory models from the synthesis library for memories. Typically, for memories a full timing black box synthesis model (has timing but no functionality) and a simulation model with both functionality and timing for verification are required.

The next step is to convert the whole design to gates using cells from the technology library. Time budgeting scripts should be developed for designs with tight timing paths and those with multi-cycle and/or functional false paths. In other words, time budget scripts for design "C" must be created for synthesis. The other designs can be synthesized to gates with minimal constraints such as clock period, approximate drives and loads and dont_touch_network on clocks specified. Designs which are instantiated more than once must be uniquified so that multiple references of the design are created. These separate references are then synthesized independently based upon their immediate environment. The overall synthesis process can be automated using "make" files.

The RAM BIST logic is instantiated in the design and should not be modified during synthesis. Hence, it must be "dont_touched" during synthesis. (dont_touch is the Synopsys DC attribute that ensures that the synthesis tool does not modify a design). Sub-design "IP" is a netlist targeted to the same technology library which is being re-used in this ASIC. Hence the dont_touch methodology must be used for the sub-design A3 in design A.

After synthesizing all the blocks in the design, the next step is to derive constraints for each of the sub-designs in context of the top level constraints and the logic in the fan-in and fan-out of the sub-design. This can be done from the "CORE" level using the characterize command after integrating the gate level netlists for all the blocks in the design.

The newly derived timing constraints for the sub-designs can then used to synthesize the blocks beginning with the RTL. At this juncture, the derived scripts using "characterize" can be manually updated to modify existing constraints or to specify additional path exception information. After this synthesis step, static timing analysis must be performed on the design at the TOP level to identify any paths which are violating the setup constraints. Information obtained from static timing analysis can be used to update the characterize scripts to over-constrain the paths or specify more accurate information.

Hierarchical compile strategies can be used for designs "D" and "A" because the synthesis run-times are acceptable for these blocks. Design "B" consists of memories (which are dont_touched) and two other sub-designs. Depending on the available computing resources (CPU and memory) and acceptable synthesis run times, the two sub-design instances "B1" and "B5" could either be synthesized together or independently after deriving a characterized script for each.

Once the design converges to meeting timing, the next step is to stitch the scan cells in the design. At this stage the netlist is ready for floorplanning and placement. Then, more accurate net load information, net and cell timing numbers (SDF) are then back-annotated from the physical domain to fix any design rule constraints and hold violations in the design. Two sets of SDF files should be available after floorplanning, one for the worst case operating conditions and another for best case operating conditions. The worst case SDF file can be used to fix setup violations, while the best case SDF file is used to fix hold violations. With recent developments the Synopsys Design Compiler is capable of fixing both setup and hold violations in the same synthesis run using worst and best case timing information. This avoids any issues with the timing of the design not converging when fixing setup and hold violations in different synthesis runs. The next step involves routing of the design. This is followed by parasitic extraction and back-annotation of information based on actual routing information as discussed in chapter 1.

4.10 Datapath Synthesis

Logic synthesis and traditional place and route are good for random logic but produce unacceptable results for large datapath logic. Datapath designs are too large to optimize at the Boolean level and place and route tools can't capitalize on the underlying regularity. Parameterized designs like n-bit adder, n-bit multiplier, n-words* m-bits memory, are amenable to quick compact layout with predictable timing because of their arrayed structure.

Any attempt to use conventional logic placement and route tools for these kinds of designs would typically result in an increase in die size and less predictable timing. Therefore, these designs are often realized from custom layout by expert layout designers. Custom layout however can be extremely time consuming (of the order of several months) and requires both datapath and custom design expertise. Moreover, these layouts are limited in their ability to be re-used, because a 10-bit custom adder cannot be directly used for a 12-bit adder required in a new design. Thus, an alternate approach that does not adversely affect time to market and can help meet timing, area and power constraints is required. Datapath and memory compiler tools aim to address this need. These tools use the arrayed structure of designs to do compact layouts in a matter of hours. More importantly, they often result in areas comparable to manual layouts.

Commercial Datapath Compilers use a predefined RTL component library of Datapath cores, such as adders, multipliers, shift registers, etc. These tools take advantage of the regularity of the datapath structures and use the predefined bit slice datapath components (also called leaf cells) which are connected together during the synthesis of the datapath logic. Datapath logic can be described either using Schematic capture or a HDL netlist consisting of bit-slice components from a library. Alternately, tools which synthesize datapath logic using standard cell library components instead of pre-optimized bit slice components, are also commercially available. However, the regularity of the datapath logic is lost during the synthesis process and can result in a scattered layout unless grouped and constrained during placement and route.

A third approach used by some design houses is a "home-brewed" datapath solution. In this approach, the datapath logic is generated by instantiating in HDL or using Synopsys DesignWare libraries (a technology independent synthesizable library), special datapath cells from the conventional logic synthesis technology library. The netlist of the datapath logic is then processed by a datapath compiler to generate an optimal layout taking advantage of the arrayed structures [3]. These tools then generate a placement netlist in a format acceptable to the placement and route tool (e.g., DEF for Cadence tools Cell3/Silicon Ensemble).

4.10.1 Datapath Synthesis Design Flow

The fundamental requirement prior to datapath synthesis is that the design be partitioned up-front into datapath and control logic. Datapath tools can then be used for the structured blocks while conventional logic synthesis tools can be used for control logic. i.e bottom-up for datapath and top-down for control logic. As a final step, the control logic, the datapath logic, I/O pads, JTAG logic and memories if any, can be integrated together to generate a full-chip netlist.

Figure 4.12 shows the design flow using Datapath synthesis. The design flow is identical to the conventional logic synthesis based flow. In other words, consider the datapath block as a sub-design in the full-chip design that is synthesized, verified, and placed and routed independently. The RTL description for the full-chip design includes a black box description (as a place holder) for the datapath block. The RTL description (or schematic) for the datapath block is fed to a datapath synthesis tool. The output of the datapath synthesis tool is a placement optimized netlist for the datapath block. This netlist is then integrated with the full-chip netlist generated from logic synthesis as shown in Figure 4.12.

The integration of the datapath logic with the rest of the design (control logic, memory blocks, IOs etc.) is the final step in the "chip integration" process. Alternately, it is also possible to integrate the datapath logic into the rest of the design at the GDSII level. In other words, the datapath logic is placed and routed independently and integrated into the rest of the design at the layout level instead of integration at the netlist level.

At each stage in the design flow the required models should be available. For behavioral simulation the behavioral models for Datapath library components (such as adders, multipliers) must be made available. For static timing analysis, the netlist for datapath connectivity, the SDF file with accurate cell and interconnect delays at leaf cell level, and the timing models for leaf cells are required.

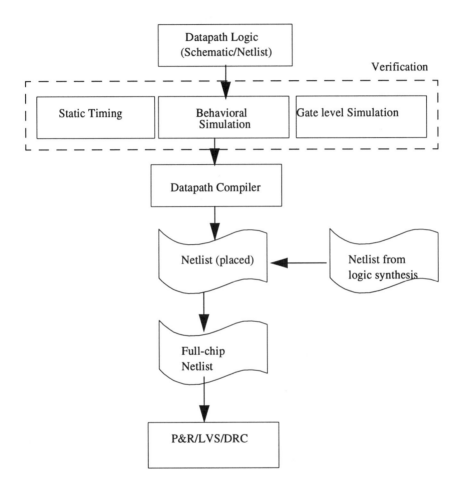

Figure 4.12 Datapath Synthesis Flow

Similarly, for gate level simulation the netlist, the SDF with accurate cell and interconnect delays at leaf cell level and the functional and timing models for leaf cells are required. Finally, for LVS, the transistor models for the leaf cells are required.

4.11 Methodology Audit

1. Are all the outputs in the different blocks in the design registered? This helps in better estimating timing between designs.

2. Are the finite state machines grouped and optimized separately? This can help improve synthesis results.

3. Have the sequential and the combinational parts of the state machine been separated? This makes debugging a lot easier.

4. Have point to point delays been specified for the different asynchronous paths?

5. Has the design been efficiently partitioned with no glue logic at the top level of the core? At the core level, the design should have only sub-designs and no glue logic.

6. Does the netlist contain unwanted latches? This happens when case statements or nested if statements are not fully defined. Besides, ensure that all signals are initialized.

7. Has an estimated skew been specified when identifying the clock ports and their respective clock periods? It is advisable to do this in order build in some margin for clock skews during the synthesis process.

8. Are false paths and multi-cycle paths identified in the synthesis scripts? If not, synthesis will spend wasteful effort in optimizing non-critical paths.

9. Has the use of available macros (such as DesignWare modules) been considered? Several basic building blocks are available in the form of re-usable, technology independent, parametrizable modules. Using these can help speed up the design process as well as improve the quality of synthesis results.

10. Are Make files used to automate the synthesis process? This also requires the usage of a well-defined directory structure for the netlist, source HDL, timing reports etc.

CHAPTER 5

Static Timing Analysis

Static Timing Analysis (STA) is an effective methodology for verifying the timing characteristics of a design without the use of test vectors. This chapter describes the methodology for verifying and fixing timing violations using STA. Several commercial static timing tools (refer to Appendix A) are available. Through simple examples, the concepts and methodologies used for static timing are illustrated in this chapter. The examples described in this chapter use the Synopsys DesignTime. However, the concepts are applicable to all static timing analysis tools in general.

This chapter is organized as follows. First, we describe the limitations of current verification methodologies. Then, we discuss the static timing analysis based design methodology. This is followed by an in-depth discussion on the methodology for specifying clocks and constraints for pre-layout synthesis and timing analysis. All static timing concepts are described by means of simple examples. Then, a list of command used in three commercial STA tools, namely, PrimeTime, Pearl and Motive are provided. The rest of the chapter covers a discussion on timing models and post-layout timing analysis. Finally, the top ten static timing methodology queries have been listed.

5.1 The Verification Bottleneck

As the semiconductor industry strives to achieve "system on a chip", conventional verification techniques like logic simulation are proving to be inadequate. As designs get larger, the task of testing all the timing paths using logic simulation is becoming too time consuming. Further, it requires thousands of vectors which take several hours of simulation time using conventional simulators. These limitations are more pronounced, especially, in designs over 100K gates. Thus, as the designs become larger and process technologies smaller, conventional techniques are faced with serious limitations. At smaller process geometries the delays due to interconnect capacitances are a big portion of the total cell delay. It is important to do more iterations of timing analysis—during initial synthesis, floor-planning, and layout. Since simulation run-times may be of the order of several days, it is not feasible to do several iterations of timing analysis for large designs with this approach. This implies the need for more sophisticated tools. The EDA industry has chosen to tackle this problem of verification by separating functional verification from timing verification. In other words, the limitations of the conventional event-driven logic simulation are being addressed, using Static Timing Analysis (for timing verification) and Cycle-based simulation (for functional verification).

There are two factors that influence successful analysis of timing in synchronous designs, namely, Methodology and Tools. A good methodology is based on identifying and fixing timing problems as early as possible in the design cycle. As suggested by the title of this book, while tools are constantly evolving to meet design needs, the design methodology is critical to the overall success of the design project. Thus, when developing a timing analysis methodology, it must be done with the entire design flow including, clock-tree synthesis, parasitics extraction, delay calculation and logic synthesis in perspective.

5.2 Static Timing Analysis vs. Logic Simulation

Static timing analysis is a technique used to determine all the possible timing violations including—setup, hold, recovery, removal and pulse width—in a design, for a specified clock, without applying test vectors. Static timing analysis tools accomplish this by exhaustively tracing every possible timing path in the design, calculating delays on these paths, and reporting timing violations, if any. The static timing analysis approach typically takes a fraction of the time it takes to run logic simulation on a large design and guarantees 100% coverage of all true timing paths in the design without having to generate test vectors.

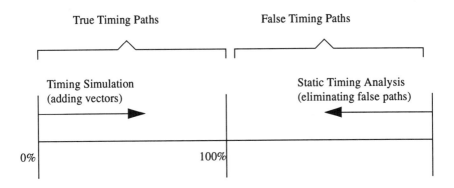

Figure 5.1 Timing analysis (simulation vs. static timing).

Static Timing tools are most appropriate for purely synchronous designs, and are often fully integrated with logic synthesis tools. Unlike logic simulation, static timing analysis does not require test vectors. Static timing analysis and logic synthesis are used in iterative loops to create logic which meets the desired timing goals. After synthesis, timing analysis is performed to generate a list of paths which violate the timing requirements. Re-synthesis of blocks with violating timing paths is done with tighter constraints in an attempt to meet timing.

The conceptual difference between simulation and static timing techniques for verification is illustrated in Figure 5.1. Clearly, the objective of timing analysis is to cover 100% of true timing paths in the design. With the simulation approach, since actual functional vectors are used, so all paths covered are true paths. Coverage of timing paths can be enhanced by increasing the number of functional vectors. It is extremely difficult to attain full coverage in large designs using the simulation approach. Section 5.4 discusses false paths in greater detail.

5.3 Static Timing Analysis Based Design Flow

Prior to exploring the use of static timing analysis in the design flow, it is important to understand some basic definitions related to static timing analysis. *Setup time* for an edge triggered sequential element is defined as the time interval before the active clock edge during which the data should remain unchanged. *Hold time* on the other hand, are defined as the time interval after the active clock edge during which the data should remain unchanged. *Recovery time* is like a setup time for asynchronous port (such as set & clear). It is a measure of the time available between the asynchronous signal going inactive to the clock going active. *Removal time* is like hold time for an asynchronous port like set, clear etc. It is a measure of time between the clock going active and the asynchronous signal going inactive. *Pulsewidth* as the name indicates is the width of a pulse. In other words, it is a measure of the time between the active and inactive states of the same signal.

In this section, a step by step design flow is described, with a special focus on identifying timing problems in designs using Static Timing analysis techniques. The intent here is to describe an approach that is independent of the static timing tool being used.

Figure 5.2 shows the design flow with specific focus on static timing analysis and its application at different stages in the design flow. The entire design and the application of Static timing analysis at different stages is as follows:

1. Static timing analysis is performed on the synthesized gate-level netlist to perform all possible timing checks in the design. Re-synthesis of the design might be required to fix timing violations detected during static timing analysis.

2. Floor-planning and placement are performed using floor-planning tools and parasitics (net capacitances and interconnect delays) are estimated. Pre-layout static timing analysis is performed using these estimated parasitics. At this stage, it might be required to re-optimize the design from the source HDL using custom wire load models.

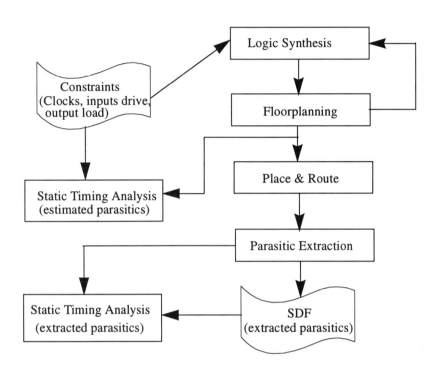

Figure 5.2 Static Timing Analysis in the ASIC Design Flow

3. Clock trees are not synthesized during logic synthesis tools. Clock
   trees are usually hand-instantiated and dont_touched during synthesis. Alternately, commercial clock tree synthesis tools are also available. Several design houses use their "home brewed" solutions for
   clock trees. The estimated impact of clock trees must be taken into
   account up-front while specifying the clocks during logic synthesis.
   Clock-tree synthesis is done during place & route to balance the
   clock skews. While the objective of clock tree synthesis is to achieve
   minimal clock skews, it is also critical that the skews assumed during logic synthesis are comparable to the actual skews after
   clock-tree synthesis, placement and routing. The numbers assumed
   during synthesis are rough estimates based on previous experience,

knowledge of the process technology etc. Static timing analysis is performed on the design after inserting the clock tree to calculate actual skews based on back annotation information.

4. Parasitics are extracted after placement and routing to obtain accurate net capacitances and resistances. The interconnect (time of flight) pin to pin delays are also obtained based on actual routing lengths and technology in the Standard Delay Format (SDF) file. This data is then used to perform post-layout static timing analysis.

5. A new netlist which includes the pre-layout netlist with the addition of the clock tree is generated. Then, static timing analysis is re-run on this netlist with actual propagation delay through clock-tree buffers and actual net and cell delays based on extracted parasitics. Any setup and hold violations detected at this stage, is fixed by in-place optimization. Some place and route tools that support a timing driven place and route flow, are also capable of performing in-place optimization.

5.4 Pre-Layout Static Timing Analysis

In this section, we discuss the methodology for specifying clocks and constraints for pre-layout synthesis and timing analysis using a simple example. We also discuss the generation and interpretation of timing reports.

Example 5.1   Simple Design with a Clock

Figure 5.3 shows an example of clocks in a design sub-module called CLKGEN. The primary clock input port has a 20 Mhz reference clock, "clkref20m". This clock is divided to generate an inverted 10 Mhz clock, "clk10mz". This example has been used throughout this chapter to illustrate static timing analysis concepts.

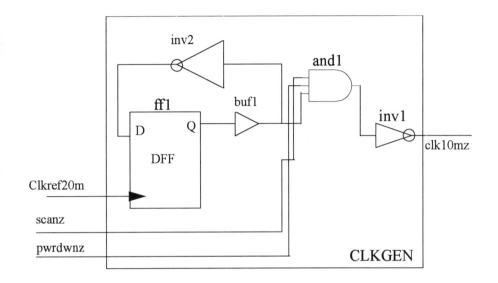

Figure 5.3 Design Showing Clocks

5.4.1   Creating Clocks Sources

The first step in providing constraints for static timing analysis involves specifying the clocks. Defining clock sources is critical for optimal synthesis and accurate static timing analysis and should be done with due diligence before logic synthesis. To avoid setup and hold violations downstream in the design cycle, the clock skew balancing strategy must also be considered prior to logic synthesis. When creating clocks for synthesis and timing analysis, it is important to accurately specify the phase and skew relationship between the clocks. For example 5.1, the clock waveform relationship is as shown in Figure 5.4.

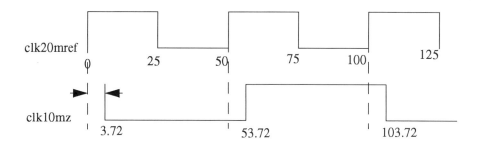

Figure 5.4 Clock Phase and Skew Relationship

Prior to defining the clocks it is essential to calculate the skew between the two clocks. The skew relationship between clk20mref and clk10mz can be obtained in Synopsys DesignTime using the following command:

```
report_timing -delay max -from {"clkgen/ff1/CLK"} -to {"clk-
gen/inv1/Z"}
```

Let us assume that a value of 3.72 is obtained for this path in our example for the fast corner library. Using the skew information these clocks can be defined with the following DesignTime commands:

```
create_clock clkref20m -name clkref20m -period 50
create_clock clkgen/clk10mz -name clk10mz -period 100 -waveform
{50 100}
```

The `set_clock_skew` command must be used to explicitly specify the skew of 3.72 ns. When doing synthesis and timing analysis for the slow corner library, clocks must be re-created with the appropriate skew value obtained by executing the `report_timing` command.

In general, synthesis must initially be performed using the slow corner library to identify setup violations. Then, timing analysis must be performed using the fast corner library. This should help detect hold violations. These violations can be fixed by re-optimization.

5.4.2   Identifying False Paths

Static timing analysis tools require that false paths be identified. These paths are those that are logically/functionally impossible. The goal in static timing analysis is to do timing analysis on all "true" timing paths. It is important to understand what "true" timing paths means. There may be several paths in a design which can never get sensitized under any input conditions. These paths are known as "false" paths. All other paths are "true" paths.

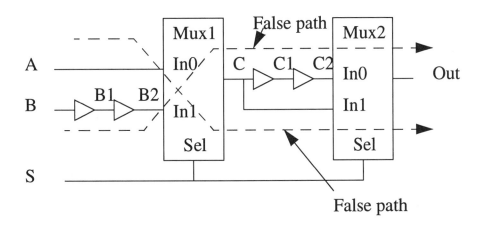

Figure 5.5 False Paths.

Figure 5.5 shows an example of false path. A cursory look at the figure shows that there are 4 timing paths through Mux1 and Mux2 as shown below:

Path1: A - C - C1 - C2 - Out

Path2: A - C - Out (through In1 of Mux2)

Path3: B - B1 - B2 - C - C1 - C2 - Out

Path4: B - B1 - B2 - C - Out (through In1 of Mux2)

Observe that since the select signal ("S") drives both the Muxes, this design can have only two possible active timing paths at any given time, namely, Path1 and Path4. When "S" is 0, Path1 is active and when "S" is 1, Path4 is active. Thus, the paths Path2 and Path4 are false paths, because they would never get sensitized for any input on "S". Hence, these paths need to be eliminated for static timing analysis.

In example 5.1 notice that the "scanz" and "pwrdownz" ports must be set to logic 1 during functional operation. This is accomplished by the Synopsys command:

```
set_logic_one   {"scanz", "pwrdownz"}
```

Thus, any paths originating from scanz or pwrdownz port must be false paths.

5.4.3   Identifying Multi-Cycle Paths

It essential that the multi-cycle paths in the design be identified both for synthesis and STA. By default, static timing tools assume timing paths to be single cycle paths unless specified otherwise. Multi-cycle paths are those paths that require more than one clock period for execution.

With the static timing analysis approach, by default, 100% of all true timing paths are covered. However, it also provides coverage for all false paths. It is critical that these false paths be identified to the static timing analysis tool. This can be accomplished in a couple of ways. One approach is to manually inspect the design and the timing reports from static timing analysis. Second approach is to identify the paths based on the knowledge of the design and its desired behavior.

5.4.4   Timing Loops

The STA tools require long run-times to detect timing loops and "break" them. Timing loops are caused due to combinational feedback loops or due to buses. If the user detects loops, it is possible to apply constraints to expedite the analysis. For example, in Motive one can use the BUS statement to group signals into a bus. This means that a transition on one signal of the bus does not cause a transition on any other signal of the same bus. This declaration guides the tool not to trace paths that are loops thereby eliminating false paths more efficiently.

Figure 5.6 shows a simple example of a combinatorial feedback loop from the output of Mux2 to the input of Mux1. STA analysis requires that this loop be broken, so the tool can avoid tracing this path. While this is a simple example, a typical design can have several such loops, many of which are extremely long and require significant run times to trace. Timing loops are common when tri-state busses are present in the design. Thus in general, timing loops need to be detected in order to improve STA run-times. While STA tools are capable of detecting and breaking timing loops, identifying them through tool-specific commands can help speed up the STA process.

In general, timing loops can be addressed by identifying the paths causing the loops (check_timing -verbose -loops command in PrimeTime). Alternately, one can use "case analysis" to disable loops (set_case_analysis command in PrimeTime). A third approach is to explicitly disable timing loops (set_disable_timing) by breaking them using tools specific commands. Two additional DesignTime commands that can assist in the analysis process are report_transitive_fanin and report_transitive_fanout.

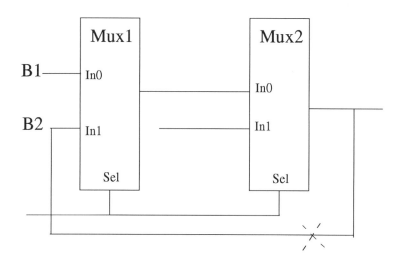

Figure 5.6 Combinational Feedback Loop

5.4.5   Clocks Trees and Skews

The clock tree network is usually hand crafted or synthesized using clock tree synthesis tools. Conventional logic synthesis tools like Synopsys DC are prevented from creating a clock tree network on all the clock sources in a design with the following command after creating clocks:

```
set_dont_touch_network all_clocks()
```

Accounting for clock skews right through the design flow and predicting possible skews in actual silicon are critical to any design project. In this section, we describe a simple example to illustrate the concept of clock skews.

Example 5.2   Detecting Hold Violations

Consider a design with two flip-flops with instance names ff1 and ff2 as shown in Figure 5.7. Between the two instances is a block of combinational logic whose total delay is 2ns. While ff1 is driven by clk20mref, ff2 is driven by clk10mz. As described in Example 5.1, clk20mref has a clock period of 50ns and clk10mz has a period of 100ns. Recall that a skew of 3.72ns exists between clk20mref and clk10mz.

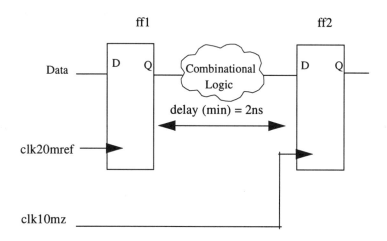

Figure 5.7 Design driven by two clocks

Consider the impact of not specifying the skew between clk20mref and clk10mz. Figure 5.8 shows the waveforms in both cases. In Case 1, the appropriate skew of 3.72ns is not declared when creating the clocks. Notice that in this case the hold violation goes undetected. On the other hand, in Case 2 the skew of 3.72ns is specified. In this case, the hold violation is detected.

Case 1:   With hold time of 1.5 ns, without clock skews we have no hold
violation. We have a hold margin of (2 -1.5) = 0.5ns

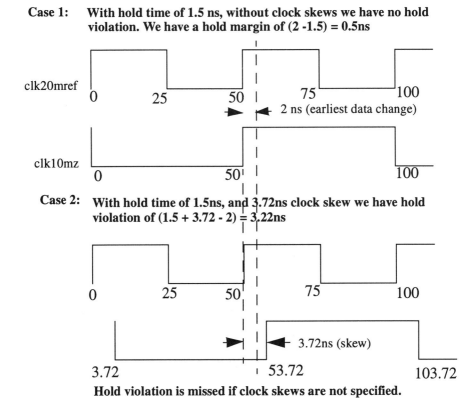

Case 2:   With hold time of 1.5ns, and 3.72ns clock skew we have hold
violation of (1.5 + 3.72 - 2) = 3.22ns

Hold violation is missed if clock skews are not specified.

Figure 5.8 Detecting Hold Violations

5.4.6   Specifying Clock Network Delays

After creating clock sources, the next step is to specify the skews
between clocks arriving at the flip-flops and propagation delays through
the clock tree buffers starting at the clock sources. Specifying the skews
at this stage is difficult, because the clock-tree has not yet been
generated. Thus, estimated values are specified for delays in the clock
network based on number of sequential elements clocked by a certain
clock source, prior experience of achievable skew targets and
knowledge of the process technology.

Example 5.3   Clock Networks

Consider the design shown in Figure 5.9. Two flip flop instances ff1 and ff2 are driven by two clocks clk20mref and clk10mz respectively. Combinational logic with a delay of 5ns exists between ff1 ad ff2. While clk20mref has a clock network delay of 4ns, clk10mz has a clock network delay of 2ns. Just as in example 5.2, clk20mref has a clock period of 50ns and clk10mz has a period of 100ns. Also, a skew of 3.72ns exists between clk20mref and clk10mz.

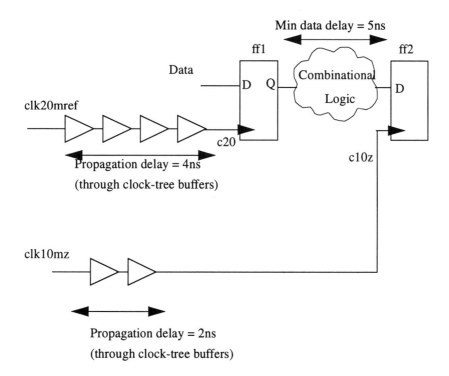

Figure 5.9 Clock Network Delay

Two possible scenarios are shown in Figure 5.10. In Case 1, the delay through clock buffers is taken into account. While in Case 2, the clock tree buffer delay is ignored. Notice that in case 1, there is no hold violation, whereas in case 2 a hold violation is detected. Hence, it is important that clock network delays be considered during timing analysis. If not, incorrect violations might be detected, while true violations might be masked.

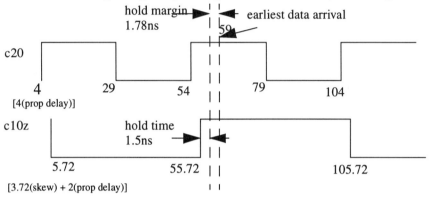

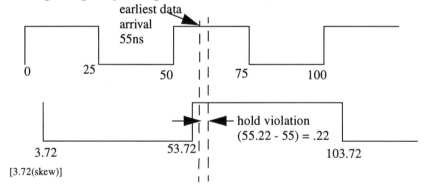

Figure 5.10 Impact of delays through clock-tree buffers.

In Example 5.3, clk20mref has a larger delay through the clock tree network of 4ns and clk10mz has a smaller delay of 2ns. As a result the rising edge of clock to ff1 (c20) arrives late at 54ns. The rising edge of clock to ff2 (c10z) arrives at 55.72ns (3.72 ns is the skew of clk10mz with respect to clk20mref and 2ns is the propagation delay through clock tree buffers of clk10mz, giving a total delay of 5.72ns). Assuming a hold time requirement of 1.5ns and minimum data path of 5ns, there is no hold violation in the above example (hold margin is 59 - (55.72 + 1.5) = 1.28ns). This is shown in the waveforms of Case 1.

However, if we were to ignore the delays through the clock buffers, then we would have obtained a hold time violation of .22ns as illustrated in waveforms of Case 2, which would have been incorrect.

In this example, there were two separate clocks with different number of levels of clock-tree buffers. But even for the same source clock, with the same number of level of buffers, there could be variances (or uncertainty) in delay for clock to reach the flip-flop clock pins. This is because the routing for all the nets is unique, resulting in different net capacitances and delays. Hence, it is important to specify both the skew and uncertainty in the clock network. The delay through the clock tree network and the uncertainty can be specified for the clocks in DesignTime with the following commands:

```
set_clock_skew -ideal -delay 4.0 -uncertainty 0.5 clk20mref
set_clock_skew -ideal -delay 2.0 -uncertainty 0.5 clk10mz
```

5.4.7   Specifying Drive on Clock Ports

Clock sources (without clock buffers during synthesis) often feed a very large number of flip-flops. Hence, the synthesis tools assumes a very large capacitance on the clock nets and the destination flip-flop pins. This would result in an extremely large input slew time from the clocks to the destination flip-flops. This in turn could lead to far from optimal synthesis results and incorrect timing analysis. To avoid this, an infinite drive must be declared on the clock sources

```
set_drive 0 clk20mref
```

In early versions of Synopsys DC it was not possible to specify a high drive on internally generated clocks. For optimal synthesis and timing analysis, one approach was to insert a fictitious cell with a very high drive on the clock sources for internally generated clocks.

However, in DC98 and later versions for the internally generated clocks, one can use the `set_clock_transition` command to implement ideal clocks. For example, to set 0 transition on an internal clock ina one can do the following:

```
create_clock ina -p 10 U1/o
set_clock_transition 0 ina
```

where o is the output pin of instance u1 and ina is an internal clock.

5.4.8   Generating and Interpreting Timing Reports

All setup and hold violations in the design can be obtained with the following DesignTime command:

```
report_constraints -all_violators -verbose
```

It is important to identify which paths barely missed setup or hold violations, because they help discover potential problem areas. One way to address this is by, increasing the uncertainty in the clock skew specification as shown below:

```
set_clock_skew -ideal -delay 4.0 -uncertainty 2.0 clk20mref
set_clock_skew -ideal -delay 2.0 -uncertainty 2.0 clk10mz
```

It is also possible to generate pin-to-pin timing using the following commands:

```
report_timing [-from <pin_name>] [-to <pin_name>]
```

Example 5.4 shows a sample timing report generated from DesignTime. This report indicates that there was a setup violation of 1.30ns for the timing path between flip-flops `countint_reg<2>` and `fxlbdatint_reg`. The first portion of the timing values gives a breakdown of the delay through the data path and the second portion that of the clock path.

Notice that the clock network delay in the report is 0. In other words, an ideal clock network is assumed unless the `-propagated` option is used when specifying the clock skew.

Example 5.4   Timing Report Generated by DesignTime

```
Startpoint: countint_reg<2>
            (rising edge-triggered flip-flop clocked by xpl125m)
  Endpoint: fxlbdatint_reg
            (rising edge-triggered flip-flop clocked by xpl125m)
  Path Group: xpl125m
  Path Type: max
```

Point	Incr	Path
clock xpl125m (rise edge)	0.00	0.00
clock network delay (ideal)	0.00	0.00
countint_reg<2>/CLK (SDFFRB)	0.00	0.00 r
countint_reg<2>/Q (SDFFRB)	1.87	1.87 f
U39/Z (AOI22)	0.79	2.66 r
U15/Z (AND2B)	1.03	3.69 r
U12/Z (AO22B)	1.21	4.89 r
U13/Z (INVB)	0.52	5.42 f
fxlbdatint_reg/D (DFFR)	0.00	5.42 f
data arrival time		5.42
clock xpl125m (rise edge)	6.00	6.00
clock network delay (ideal)	0.00	6.00
fxlbdatint_reg/CLK (DFFR)	0.00	6.00 r
library setup time	-1.89	4.11
data required time		4.11
data required time		4.11
data arrival time		-5.42
slack (VIOLATED)		-1.30

5.4.9 Data path Delay Calculation

In the timing report shown in example 5.4, the delay through the clock tree network from clock source xpl125m was assumed ideal and was thus 0ns. The CLK to Q delay of flip-flop countint_reg<2> is 1.87ns., which is followed by the delays through each gate in the data path. The time it takes for data to arrive at destination flip-flop (fxlbdating_reg) is 5.42ns.

5.4.10 Clock Path Delay Calculation

For setup violation check, static timing analysis tools look at the next rising edge of the clock (which happens at 6ns—the clock period is 6ns and there is no delay assumed through the clock network). The setup time for destination flip-flop is 1.89ns. This means that data should be stable at (6.0 -1.89) 4.11ns. Since Data path calculation shows that latest data arrives is 5.42ns, therefore there is a setup violation of (5.42 - 4.11 = -1.30) 1.30ns.

5.4.11 Summary of DesignTime Commands

All the DesignTime commands for defining the clocks and constraints for pre-layout synthesis and timing analysis are summarized below:

```
create_clock clkref20m -name clkref20m -period 50
create_clock clkgen/clk10mz -name clk10mz -period 100 -waveform
{53.72 103.72}
set_logic_one { "scanz", "pwrdownz" }
set_dont_touch_network all_clocks()
set_clock_skew -ideal -delay 4.0 -uncertainty 0.5 clk20mref
set_clock_skew -ideal -delay 2.0 -uncertainty 0.5 clk10mz
set_drive 0 clk20mref
```

5.5 PrimeTime, Motive and Pearl Commands

Synopsys PrimeTime accepts all DesignTime commands. However, we list below a summary of the essential PrimeTime commands and their application.

Table 1: PrimeTime Commands

Command	Application
set_input_delay	Arrival time for Inputs
set_output_delay	Required output time
set_driving_cell	Information about cell driving port.
set_input_transition	Transition time of input ports
create_clock	Identifying clocks (including waveforms, period, etc)
set_clock_uncertainity	Uncertainty or margin of error (can be identified as an option to create_clock)
set_clock_latency	Defines latency of clock (can be identified as an option to create_clock)
set_capacitance	External capacitive load on port.
set_wire_load_model	Wire load model to be used
set_max_transition	Requirements for transition time.
set_fanout_load	Load on pins due to external loads.
set_false_path	Timing exception implying "dont care" on path
set_multicycle_path	Identifying paths which require more than one clock cycle
set_port_fanout_number	Identifies number of port fanouts. Can be an option to set_wire_load_model.

PrimeTime and DesignTime are closely integrated with the Design Compiler logic synthesis tool. Hence, several of the synthesis constraints are directly applicable in both PrimeTime and DesignTime. On the other hand, Motive was built as a stand alone static timing analysis tool independent of the logic synthesis environment. Hence, some DesignTime and PrimeTime commands such as `set_wire_load_model`, `set_max_transition`, `set_fanout_load` have no direct equivalent in Motive.

Table 2: Motive Commands

Command	Application

`TIN NET in[0] REF clock`
`EDGE R RISE 1.0 1.0 FAL`
`1.0 1.0`
	Specifying Input delay (where in[0] and clock are net names)

`TSH NET out[3] REF`
`clock EDGE R SETUP 1.0`
`1.0 HOLD 1.0 1.0( )`
	Specifying output delay (where out[3] and clock are net names)

`Group G0 REFDEF clock T`
`CYCDEF Up 0 0 DOWN 5 5`
`CYCLE 10`
`ENDREF`
	Defining the clock

`CLKGEN G0 G0`	Clock uncertainty
`netload`	Specifying load on outputs.

`MCP CONST {`
`      FROM U045 A`
`      TO U124 B`
`}`
	Identifying false paths (where U045 and U124 are instances, A and B pin names)

`MCP SETUP 1 HOLD 1 {`
`   FROM U9 Q`
`   TO U2 D`
`}`
	Defining multi-cycle path (where U9 and U2 are instances, D and Q pin names)

Table 3: Pearl Commands

Command	Application
`Input a clk ^ 5 10 5 10`	Specifying input delays Input pins clk clk_edge rise_min rise_max fall_min fall_max
`Constraint out clk ^ 8 0 1 0`	Specifying ouput delays Constraint output_ports clk clk_edge rise_setup fall_setup rise_hold_hold
`Clock -cycle_time 10 clk1 0 5`	Creating clocks
`Clock -cycle_time 10 -skew 0.5 clk1 0 5`	Defining skews for clock sources
`DriverStrength pins rise_min rise_max fall_min fall_max`	Specifying the driving cell
`SetNodeCapacitance bushold 0.5`	Specifying capacitance
`Constant nets value or BlockPath [-nested] [-edges] [-max_paths count] from_net [nets...] to_net`	Identifying false paths
`MultiCyclePath -setup 2 -from_pins R1/CLK - to_pins R2/D`	Specifying multicycle paths

5.6 Delay Calculation

The accuracy of cell io-path delays, an input to the static timing analysis tool, depends entirely on the technology library. A timing model contains description of timing properties of a cell that a delay calculator tool uses to model the cell's timing behavior. Delay calculation is the process of determining actual values for the timing properties of each occurrence of a cell in a design. These values are then fed to a static timing analysis tool for calculating timing violations. Alternately, Delay calculation tools are sometimes built into static timing analysis tools.

The most widely used form of expressing timing equations in a technology library is the look-up table format. These tables contain delay information for different input slew and output capacitive loading. This information is used for calculating cell io-path delay values and output slew time values. As we move to smaller process geometries, it is important that timing models are capable of differentiating between active and passive loads. Currently, logic synthesis library model for output capacitive load does not differentiate between interconnect and gate-loads.

In addition to the accuracy of the library, it is important that the delay calculator take the following into account: R/C effects, non-linear dependency of delay on load capacitance, dependency of delay on input slew, cells in parallel to increase drive and additional load of the non-driving outputs (tri-state net) in the total load capacitance.

5.7 Post-Layout Timing Analysis

After layout, the following files are of interest to timing analysis:

1. ECO (Engineering Change Order) File: This contains the clock-tree buffers inserted to meet clock constraints. Incorporating these buffers into the original netlist can be a difficult task. Hence, several design houses choose not to add the buffers during place and route. Instead, they choose to generate their own hand crafted clock trees which are added to the netlist prior to place and route.

2. SDF file: This contains the Interconnect delays (time-of-flight pin-to-pin delays) based on the actual routing lengths. The SDF file also contains cell delays. However, when performing STA using DesignTime, the tool is capable of calculating cell delays based on extracted capacitances on the nets in the design.

3. Net capacitance file: This file contains extracted net capacitances in the form of `set_load` commands for Design Compiler.

After back annotation of layout data, timing analysis is essentially a two step process. Firstly, the setup violations must be detected using the slow corner library. Then, the hold violations must be detected using the fast corner library. The DesignTime commands to load the design, interconnect (time of flight) delays, and net load capacitances are as follows:

```
read -f edif TOP.edif  /* Design with back-annotated
clock-trees) */
read_timing -f sdf TOP.SDF /* Interconnect delays only */
current_design TOP
include TOP.dc    /* Net load capacitance file (set_load state-
ments). */
```

After back-annotation, the clock constraints and specifications now have to be re-defined to take into account the actual propagation delays through the clock tree buffers, with actual net load capacitances. These constraints for the example 5.1 are summarized below:

```
create_clock clkref20m -name clkref20m -period 50
create_clock clkgen/clk10mz -name clk10mz -period 100 -waveform
{53.72 103.72}
/*set_clock_skew -delay 3.72 can also be used */
set_logic_one { "scanz", "pwrdownz" }
set_dont_touch_network all_clocks()
set_clock_skew -propagated clk20mref     /* post-layout */
set_clock_skew -propagated clk10mz       /* post-layout */
```

There are two important issues one must be aware of at this stage. First, the clock skews are now no longer estimated. At this stage, the actual clock skews based on back-annotated clock-tree buffers and parasitics are available. Notice the -propagated switch in the set_clock_skew statements.

5.7.1 Addressing Post-Layout Timing Issues

1. Use the `report_timing` from the pins corresponding to clock sources (e.g. `report_timing -from clkgen/clk10mz` in example 5.1) to get a feel for the worst clock skews for clock signals generated by the same or different clock sources.

2. Generate a table of pairs of clock sources which interact in timing paths in the design. A knowledge of interacting clock pairs can assist in clock-skew balancing that needs to be done across clock trees.

3. Editing the netlist to insert buffers and higher drive cells. This works provided changes are minimal. This method is extremely error prone and must be avoided if possible.

4. In order to meet timing constrains after back-annotation, perform in-place optimization (IPO), on the design either in the synthesis environment or using the place and route tools.

5. If the timings violations can't be fixed by IPO or by minor hand edits, it might be required to re-synthesize the design (or sub-designs) from the source HDL. In such cases, ensure that custom wire load models (wire load models generated from back-annotated information) are used during re-synthesis. Alternately, it might also be possible to meet timing by incremental synthesis on the existing netlist using the back-annotation information.

5.8 Methodology Audit

1. Do you follow naming conventions to identify signals such as reset, set, load, gated clocks etc. Following such conventions significantly helps in the debug process.

2. Have you considered skews between clock sources in a multi-clock designs for STA and synthesis?

3. Have you ignored skews since your design has only low frequency clocks? Clock skews between source and destination flip-flops, even on low frequency clocks can result in hold time violations.

4. In the STA tool, did you ensure that the clock network delays are considered after back-annotation? (e.g., "-propagated" option must be used in DesignTime). For example, by default DesignTime assumes ideal (no delay) delays through the clock network.

5. Do you use the slow corner library for setup violation checks and fast corner library for hold violation checks?

6. Does your place and route tool balance skews between different clock-tree networks?

7. During synthesis do you ensure to specify high drive on external and internal clock sources?

8. During STA do you ensure that all the false paths and the multi-cycle paths been identified?

9. When back-annotating SDF into the STA tool do you check the reports to ensure that all the timing arcs in the design have been back-annotated?

10. Do you perform static timing analysis at the module level? This makes the static timing analysis process simpler once you get to a higher level in the design hierarchy.

CHAPTER 6

Test Concepts and Methodologies

With decrease in feature sizes, built-in test capabilities is fast becoming a must in most designs. Statistics have shown that the cost of detecting a defective chip increases by 10X from the chip level to the board level and finally to the system level. Hence, the overhead due to test logic in terms of area and timing is fast becoming justifiable. Full-scan, partial-scan, I_{DDQ} and built-in self test (BIST) are the four different available test methodologies. Of these scan techniques are the most commonly used. This chapter is devoted to Test concepts and methodologies. The primary intent is to provide the reader an in-depth understanding of the issues involved in test synthesis and techniques to address them.

This chapter is organized as follows. First, the different scan methodologies and scan styles are introduced, followed by Test Protocol sequence. Then, scan synthesis, re-ordering, boundary scan synthesis and Automatic Test Pattern Generation (ATPG) are described. This is followed by a discussion on Test Design Rule Checkers and techniques to fix test design rule violations. The next section covers the sequence of steps that make up the test protocol. The last section lists a series of methodology audit queries focused on test synthesis.

6.1 Scan Methodologies and Scan Styles

The first step in test synthesis involves choosing the scan methodology and the scan style. Full Scan and Partial Scan are the two test methodologies widely used in the industry. In general, scan cells are added and connected together to form a scan chain. This helps control ("controllability") the internal sequential nodes in the design to pre-defined values, capture data values in internal sequential cells and propagate ("observability") these values through the scan chain. These propagated values are then verified against an expected set of values for these nodes.

The ATPG algorithm used is determined by the Test Methodology chosen. For example, Full Scan implies the use of a combinational ATPG algorithm. In full scan, all sequential cells that do not violate any test design rules are connected together in the form of a scan chain. The sequential cells which violate any test design rules cannot be included in the scan chain. When sequential cells violate any test design rules they are treated as black boxes by the ATPG algorithm. When such black boxes are encountered by the ATPG algorithm it assumes that the cell propagates an unknown. These black boxes are different from conventional black boxes in the technology library. A conventional black-box is usually a library cell that does not have its functionality described in the technology library.

Partial Scan test methodology implies a sequential ATPG algorithm. In partial scan test methodology, scan insertion is constraint-driven. In other words, based on the timing, area or fault coverage constraints provided and their relative priority, a percentage of all the sequential cells in the designs are replaced with scan cell equivalents.

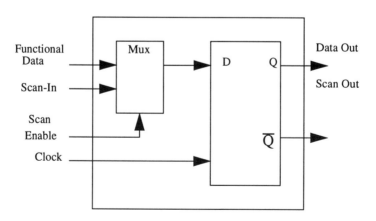

Figure 6.1 Multiplexed Flip-Flop Scan Style

Sequential ATPG, in general, is more complicated since it is required to keep track of the history of values of sequential cells not on the scan chain. Thus, sequential ATPG is more memory and compute intensive. The most obvious advantage of Partial Scan methodology is that the scan selection algorithm takes into account the impact of timing and area on scan synthesis.

The nature of scan cells that are used to replace sequential cells in the design during scan insertion, determines the Scan Style. The widely used commercial scan styles include, multiplexed flip flop, clocked scan and level sensitive scan design (LSSD). ASIC vendors may support all the scan styles or a subset of them. Of all the available scan styles multiplexed flip-flop is the simplest and the most widely used scan style. This is however, not applicable for latch-based designs, since it does not have a scan equivalent for latches. Figure 6.1 shows a multiplexed flip-flop scan cell. Replacing sequential elements with the multiplexed flip-flop scan cells causes an additional setup delay due to the multiplexer and a corresponding increase in area.

Clocked Scan is another possible scan style for edge triggered flip-flops. Latches on the other hand, do not have scan equivalents. Clocked scan cells have a separate test clock instead of a scan enable pin. This makes clocked scan very attractive for partial scan test methodologies since there is no clock gating logic required for sequential cells that are not on the scan chain. (Figure 6.2). The data_in and clock ports are used in normal mode while the test_in and scan_clk ports are used in the scan mode of operation.

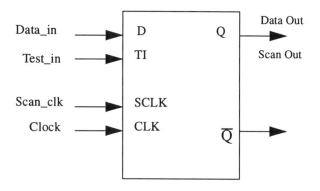

Figure 6.2 Clock Scan Style

There are several possible flavors of LSSD cells. In general, these cells are considered as scan replacements for both flip-flops and level sensitive latches. They use non-overlapping master and slave clocks for shifting in data into the scan chain as shown in Figure 6.3. Note that non-overlapping clock pulses are needed on CLK and CLKB to register either the functional data or the test input. That is, CLK and CLKA are master clocks, while CLKB is a slave clock.

When it comes to modeling capability of most EDA tools, the multiplexed flip-flop scan style is by far the easiest to model. On the other hand, scan styles that have more than one clock are difficult to model. Hence, for such scan styles scan replacement is usually based on some pre-defined attribute.

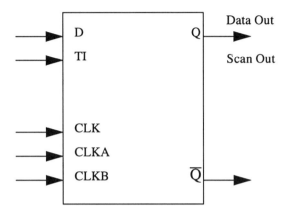

Figure 6.3 LSSD Scan Style

6.2 Test Protocol Sequence

The Test protocol sequence is the series of steps performed for each test pattern during testing. The test protocol may differ marginally from vendor to vendor but the basic steps are identical. In general, each test pattern goes through the following steps: Scan Shift, Parallel Cycles and Capture Cycle.

During the Scan Shift phase all the scan chains are initialized to a known value and their values observed during shift-out. Since this process is serial, the number of cycles required for the Scan Shift phase is determined by the length of the longest scan chain in the design. For example, if the longest scan chain length is 1600 and the design has 2000 test patterns, the total tester cycles required will exceed 32,00000 cycles. Hence, one must consider using the maximum allowable number of scan chains and try to balance them. Having approximately equal number of scan cells per scan chain is called balancing. Depending on the scan style being used, during scan shift you may have to assert the scan_enable pin for multiplexed_flip_flop scan style, or use the test clock pin for clocked scan. Also in order to save test cycles, the scan shift in and the scan shift out occur simultaneously. This means that while you are shifting in data to initialize the scan chain in one test pattern, you can shift out data captured, into the scan chain from the previous test pattern.

After the "Scan Shift" phase all the scan cells on the scan chain will have been initialized. In the "Parallel Cycle" phase values are applied to all primary inputs as well as bi-directional ports being used as inputs in this pattern. Then, the primary outputs and bi-directional ports being used as outputs in this test pattern are strobed.

Finally capture the data on the data pins of the scan cells in the scan chain in the "Capture Cycle" using a single clock pulse. This is the parallel capture cycle. The data captured into the scan chain in this cycle is shifted out during the next Scan Shift phase. The above sequence is followed for each of the test patterns. The concepts described above are generic and some ASIC vendors may have different order of the above phases.

6.3   Test Design Rule Checker

The fundamental objective of test insertion is to make the design both, controllable and observable. The nature of the design directly impacts the controllability and observability, and hence the testability of the design. The test design rule checker checks for any characteristics which can affect the controllability and observability of the design. These characteristics are called test violations. The test design rule checker is typically run on a gate-level netlist of the design. However, test design rule checkers at the RTL level are currently being explored by EDA vendors. In this section, we describe some of the common checks performed by test design rule checker and their impact on fault coverage when violated.

6.3.1   Uncontrollable Clocks

On the tester, it is essential that all the clock pins of sequential cells be controllable from the primary inputs. Hence, for gated clocks and internally generated divided clocks, the test design rule checker will flag a violation and will not be able to include all the scan cells clocked by the violated clock on the scan chain. This violation should be addressed. One approach is to add a multiplexer prior to the test clock primary input. Thus, the test clock is used in the test mode while the gated clock is used in the functional mode. Figure 6.4 shows an example of a clock which is uncontrollable since it is internally generated.

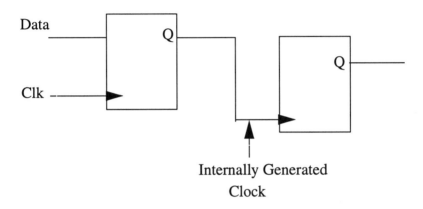

Internally Generated
Clock

Figure 6.4 Uncontrollable Clock

6.3.2   Uncontrollable Asynchronous Reset Lines

During scan shift, the asynchronous pins should be made inactive so as not to corrupt the data that is shifted in. Hence, all the asynchronous pins of sequential elements must be directly controllable from the primary inputs. The mux technique discussed for uncontrollable clocks can also be used here. Figure 6.5 shows an asynchronous reset line that is uncontrollable since it is internally generated.

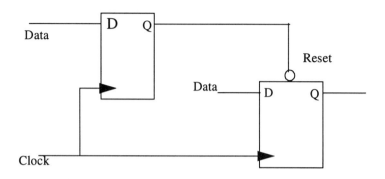

Figure 6.5 Uncontrollable Asynchronous Lines

6.3.3   Uncontrollable Scan Cell Violation

These violations indicate that the violating scan cells cannot be controlled to a known value through scan shifting. In general, these violations must be addressed. However, depending on the cause of the violation, several different techniques can be used to address these violations. In this section, we discuss some of the common design scenarios under which these violations occur and describe ways to address them.

Scenario 1: Very often, bi-directional ports are used for scan-in purposes. This can be an issue when necessary logic has not been added to configure the bi-directional ports explicitly in the input mode during scan shift. This problem can be addressed by adding necessary combinational logic such that when in scan shift mode the bi-directional ports are always in the input mode. Figure 6.6 illustrates the configuration of bi-directional ports as scan ports.

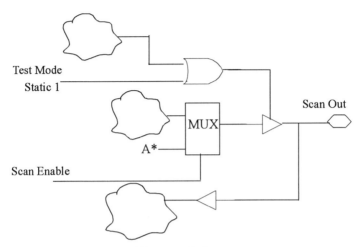

*Connected to last scan cell in scan chain

Figure 6.6 Configuration of Bi-directional Ports as Scan-Ports

Scenario 2: Clocks of the violating cells are not controllable from the primary inputs. This problem can be tackled by adding a mux to bypass the logic on the clock path as described in section 6.3.1

Scenario 3: Another potential cause for violations is when mixing clock edges on the same scan chain. For example, a Return to Zero clock that has positive edge triggered flip-flops before the negative edge triggered flops, causes all the negative edge triggered flops to be scan uncontrollable. This can be fixed by either changing the clock waveform to Return to One or moving all the negative edge triggered flip-flops before the positive edge triggered flip-flops in the scan chain.

6.3.4   Violation when Scan Cells are not Observable

Most often, this violation occurs when using both edges of the clock in the functional mode of the design. If this is the case, one approach is to use the same polarity of the clock in the test mode through a conditional inversion when the ASIC is in the test mode. Figure 6.7 shows clock polarity inversion using an exclusive OR gate.

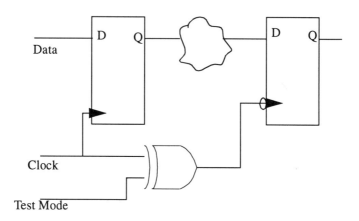

Figure 6.7 Inversion of Clock Polarity

6.3.5   No Scan Equivalent Cells Condition

This condition occurs when there are no valid scan equivalent cells in the technology library for the sequential cells in the design. Cells without scan equivalents in the technology library are not included in the scan chain. The only option here is to update your technology library with appropriate scan cells. Alternately, one must ensure that sequential cells without scan equivalents are not used during initial synthesis.

6.4 Scan Chain Synthesis

Scan chain synthesis involves replacing sequential cells with scan cell equivalents and connecting them together in a scan chain. This step is done only after a gate level netlist has been generated using a specific technology library. This is a two step process. The first step involves logic synthesis to generate a technology specific netlist. This is followed by the scan insertion step. It is important that all the test design rule checker violations are addressed prior to entering the scan insertion step. Further, after scan insertion the netlist will have to be optimized to meet the timing delays introduced due to scan insertion.

An alternate approach is called one pass synthesis. In this approach, all sequential cells are replaced by scan cells during the synthesis phase itself. However, the scan cells are not connected together to form a scan chain. The process of connecting them together must be done after the synthesis or after placement. The intent here is to address the issue of additional delays introduced due to scan insertion, during the initial synthesis phase. However, this strategy does have certain limitations. For instance, in this approach, the process of test design rule checking is done after the scan cells are already in the netlist. In the conventional flow it is always desirable that all test design violations be addressed prior to scan insertion. On the other hand, it reduces optimization iterations by accounting for scan during the initial synthesis phase.

Figure 6.8 shows the complete test synthesis flow as a part of the overall synthesis process (also known as one-pass synthesis).

As a normal practice, spare cells are usually inserted into the design for ECO purposes. This provides the flexibility of fixing functional and timing problems through metal turns only, as opposed to "all-layer" turns. Spare cells are a collection of elements (combinational and sequential) which are instantiated in the design by the user. Alternately, they can also be hard macro blocks provided by the ASIC vendor. The sequential cells in the spare blocks could be either included in the scan chain or not depending on the fault coverage impact. However, ATPG must be re-run for the design after an ECO that uses the spare cells. Using cells from the spare block to fix functional and timing problems can be a difficult task depending upon the location of the block, proximity to the problem area in the layout of the design etc.

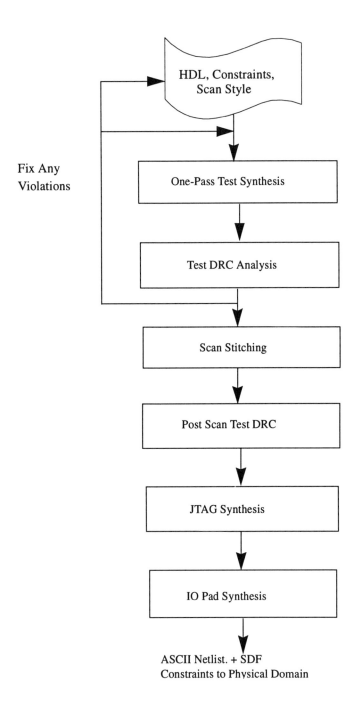

Figure 6.8 Test Synthesis Flow

The strategy for stitching scan chains in a design can be top-down, bottom-up or a combination of both. EDA tools commonly support all of these flows. Top-down scan insertion involves stitching up all scan chains from the top level of the design. Bottom-up scan synthesis involves connecting scan cells starting with the base level blocks and moving up the hierarchy. In some scenarios one may have to use combination of both these techniques. One example of this is when trying to incorporate an existing sub-module with a built-in scan chain.

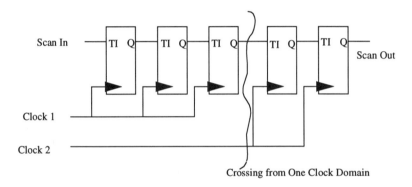

Figure 6.9 Mixing Clocks on a Scan Chain

Figure 6.9 illustrates a scenario showing clock mixing on a scan chain. In general, it is recommended that scan cells clocked by different clock domains and clock edges not be mixed together on the same scan chain. However, this might not always be feasible. For example, when the number of scan chains supported by the tester is less than the number of clock domains, then, mixing of clock domains on a single scan chain becomes inevitable. Another example, is when the number of scan cells on each of the clock domains differs significantly. Since testing time is directly proportional to the length of the longest scan chain, balancing the scan chains is essential. In such cases, in order to balance the scan chains it is required to mix clock domains on the scan chain. The primary motivation for balancing the scan chains is to reduce the test time. Automatic balancing of scan chains is a feature commonly available in EDA tools.

Each clock source should be treated as a different clock domain. Two clocks could have the same period and waveform but they should still be treated as different clock domains. This is because the clock tree and skew numbers for each clock will be different and dependent on the load and topology of sequential cells. Different clock domains in a design could have different clock skews and delays. This could cause hold violations when mixing clock domains on a scan chain. Also, different branches of the same clock domain could have different skew and delay numbers. One approach to address this issue is by adding delay cells to fix these hold violations. But this is very much dependent on the clock tree insertion delay and skew numbers.

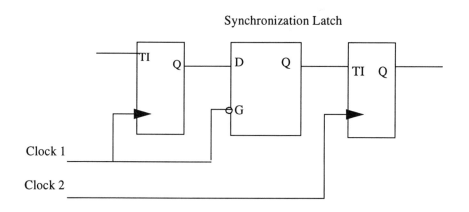

Figure 6.10 Synchronization Latch

Synchronization latches also commonly known as lockup latches are widely used in the industry to address hold/race conditions on scan chains. Synchronization latches are automatically synthesized when crossing clock domains or different branches of the same clock domain on a scan chain. Hence, when mixing scan cells of different clock domains, on the same scan chain, it is important to ensure that the interaction of clock domains is minimized. Figure 6.10 shows a synchronization lockup latch being used between two scan cells with different clocks. Note that the lock up latch mechanism can handle upto half a clock cycle of skew.

6.5 Scan Re-Ordering

In the logical domain, there is no concept of physical location information. Hence, the scan stitching in the logical domain is typically alphanumeric within a design. Physical domain environments such as those in placement and route tools have the placement and congestion information available but no test design rule checker information. Capabilities exist in the physical domain to reorder scan chains based on scan cell location and routing congestion information. Test design rule checker information is provided to the physical domain to guarantee functionally working scan chains after reordering.

Similarly, scan re-ordering capabilities exist in the logical domain based on the physical location information of the scan cells. This information is provided to the logical domain via PDEF 2.0 and subsequent versions. PDEF (Physical Design Exchange Format) is an industry standard format for communicating physical cluster and cell location information between physical domain and logical domain. Scan re-ordering in the logical domain has the advantage of having the same test design rule checker information as the ATPG tool, thereby, guaranteeing functionally working scan chains after reordering. With deep sub-micron designs, the net delay component is becoming the most significant portion of the overall delay. Further, with density of designs increasing net routing significantly impacts the overall chip utilization. This implies that in order to improve area and timing results, scan chain ordering based on physical information (location, routing) is definitely required rather than the default approach of alphanumeric ordering. The goal of the scan ordering based on physical information is to reduce scan net length based on physical proximity of cells and routing channels (tracks). This ensures better routing.

For pad limited designs, sharing functional ports with scan ports is common. Sharing the scan-in and scan-out ports with functional ports reduces the test port overhead. In a multiplexed flip-flop scan style this implies the need for only one additional port for the "scan-enable" function. When using bi-directional ports for scan ports, additional logic needs to be added to configure the direction of the bi-directional ports during test.

6.6 Boundary Scan Synthesis

Boundary Scan (IEEE 1149.1) is an industry standard board level testing initiative that defines the logic added to an ASIC that ensures effective testing at the board level. It involves adding a "Boundary Scan Register" (BSR) cell on each of the functional ports of the design along with a "TAP controller". A sixteen state FSM, instruction register, 1 bit bypass register and decoding logic to decode the instruction together make up the boundary scan JTAG logic. Besides the mandatory logic such as the BSR, the IEEE 1149.1 standard defines other optional logic for added features and functionality.

The BSR cells can be connected in a shift register structure and allow the ASIC to be isolated from the external world for test purposes. This allows sampling of input values to the ASIC. Further, it allows you to drive specific values from the ASIC through the BSR chain. This capability is the key to board level testing.

The use of "Boundary Scan" logic in a design requires four additional mandatory ports and one optional port. The mandatory ports are: "TDI" (JTAG In Port), "TDO" (JTAG Out Port), "TMS" (Test Mode Select) and "TCK" (JTAG clock). The optional port is "TRST" (asynchronous JTAG reset). The timing impact of the boundary scan logic is the additional delay through the BSR cell on the ports. The BSR architecture must be based upon the requirements of the IEEE 1149.1 specifications for the supported JTAG instructions of the ASIC design.

The sequence of events involving the Boundary Scan Logic is as follows. The board level controller first uses the TMS and TCK pins to configure the TAP controller in the ShiftIR state. Then, the desired instruction is shifted into the Instruction Register (IR) which when decoded using combinational logic selects the register selected by the instruction to be connected between TDI and TDO. Then depending on the current JTAG instruction some actions need to be taken. If the instruction requires shifting in data into the selected data register, then using the TMS and TCK pins configure the TAP controller in the "Shift DR" state. For example, the "BYPASS" instruction selects the Bypass register and allows a one cycle bypass path through an ASIC.

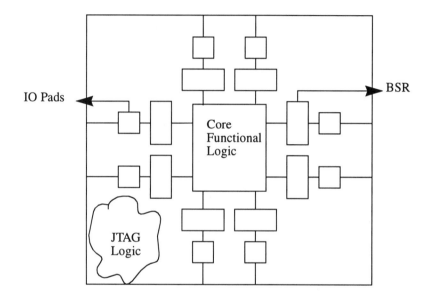

Figure 6.11 ASIC Hierarchy Partition

The "SAMPLE/PRELOAD" instruction allows the input BSRs to capture the input values and the values shifted into the BSR chains to drive the ASIC core inputs and the ASIC outputs.

Figure 6.11 shows the block diagram for an ASIC with JTAG logic, the ASIC core and the IO pads. The pad cells can be instantiated or inferred through pad synthesis. The ASIC core can include synthesized logic, embedded blocks like RAMs, ROMs, schematic generated logic etc. that comprise the complete functionality of the chip.

6.7 Automatic Test Pattern Generation (ATPG)

Once the entire design is complete, including the IO pads and JTAG logic, manufacturing test patterns can be automatically generated for the design using ATPG programs. Typically, ATPG software uses the same test design rule checker results as those used stand-alone for analysis purposes. Speed and compaction capabilities of ATPG software are two criteria commonly used in the industry to benchmark one ATPG tool against another. Speed is the CPU time required for generating the manufacturing test patterns. The compaction algorithm is measured by the total number of final test patterns for the design. Other criteria to compare ATPG tools include, handling of memories, bus holder, pull ups/down etc. ATPG tools require different kinds of information including, static values of input ports to bypass test design rule violations, tester clock period and waveform, scan ports (scan-in, scan-out etc.) and the initialization sequence to set the ASIC in test mode.

6.8 Methodology Audit

1. What scan styles are supported by the ASIC vendor? This is a fundamental issue since this determines the rules to be checked by the test design rule checker.

2. Does the current synthesis methodology being followed involve a one-pass test synthesis?

3. What is the maximum number of scan chains supported by the ASIC vendor's tester?

4. What restrictions exist on bi-directional ports? Firstly, can bi-directional ports be used as test ports? Further, how should the functional bi-directional ports be configured during scan shift phase. i.e., as inputs or outputs? In general, it is advisable to avoid using bi-directional ports as scan ports, if possible.

5. If the design has hard macro RAMs, does the ASIC vendor support RAM BIST.

6. What is the manufacturing test vector format supported for ATPG vector sign-off? Also, what sign-off simulation results are required before hand-off?

7. What is the maximum number of clocks supported by the tester? In the functional mode, the design might have several clocks. However, in the tester mode the number of clocks is limited by the number of clocks supported by the tester.

8. Is sharing of functional ports with scan ports supported by the ASIC vendor?

9. Does the back-end flow support scan chain ordering i.e., Physical Domain Based Scan Ordering? If yes, then what is the mechanism for providing the new scan chain order information to the scan synthesis and ATPG tools.

10. What are the timing requirements of the tester? These include the input application time, output strobe time, bi-directional switching time, clock period etc.

CHAPTER 7

Floor-planning and Parasitic Extraction

Several papers [19,20,21,22] have discussed the challenges in physical design targeted to DSM processes. With the migration to process technologies of 0.35um and below (in other words, deep sub-micron technologies), the disconnect between the logical domain (synthesis phase) and the physical domain (placement and routing phase) has become far more significant. To address these challenges new design methodologies are constantly being developed and deployed. For example, floor-planning has been considered to be a predominantly "back-end" activity. However, emerging floor-planning tools are now designed with the front-end logic designer in mind.

This chapter begins with a discussion on the limitations of the conventional ASIC design flow with regard to floor-planning and its role in the overall design flow. Then, we discuss the new flow which is far more "floor-planning-centric"—one in which floor-planning serves as an effective bridge between front-end and back-end tools. This is followed by a description of the different interface formats that make this flow possible. The next section describes floor-planning concepts such as grouping and regioning, manual placement of hard macros, placement of core cells, and post-placement steps. Following this, is a section on Parasitic Extraction. The remaining sections cover Clock-Tree Synthesis, the Synopsys Floorplan Manager, Physical Delay Exchange Format (PDEF) and the generation of custom wire-load models. The chapter ends with a list of top ten Methodology Audit queries.

7.1 Introduction

The design flow in the logical domain involves steps such as functional simulation at the behavioral or RTL level, behavioral synthesis, logic synthesis, test synthesis and static timing analysis. These steps are intended primarily to convert a high-level description into gates, and ensure that the functionality and timing meet the original specification. The physical domain (commonly referred to as the back-end) consists of placement of cells, routing, clock tree synthesis, parasitic extraction and layout vs. schematic verification. With the move to smaller process geometries and higher densities, the wire delay component is a significant component of the total delay on a net. Statistics show that for 0.35um technology the wire delay accounts for nearly 70% of the net delay. All of the above factors, imply that behavioral synthesis and logic synthesis phase of the design requires visibility into the physical world in terms of congestion information, net timing information etc. The Floor-planning environment is strategically placed in the design cycle to bridge this gap between the logical front end tools and the physical back end tools.

The conventional ASIC design flow for ASICs using process technologies larger than 0.35 micron, involves simulating the HDL code up-front to verify functionality, followed by logic synthesis using statistical wire-load models provided in the technology library to meet area and timing constraints. The resulting netlist is then physically placed in the specified die area. This is followed by routing the design to connect all the primitive technology cells based on the logical connectivity in the netlist. Then, using accurate net loading and placement information, net and cell delays were back-annotated to a simulator and/or static timing analysis tool to check if the timing constraints are met. If the timing constraints are not met due to the inaccuracies in the wire-load model used during the initial synthesis process, then, re-synthesis is required.

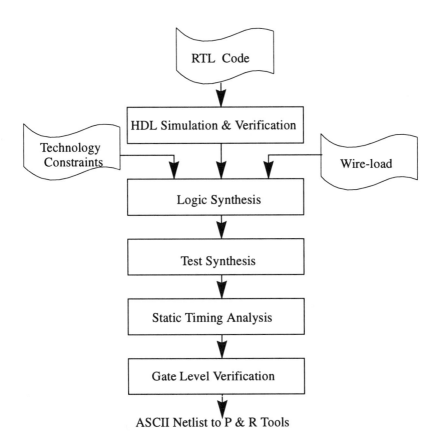

Figure 7.1 Conventional Design Flow

There are two basic limitations to this flow. Firstly, the turnaround time associated with getting R/C and timing information. In other words, in this approach, extracted parasitics are obtained only after placement and routing. This is too late in the design cycle and can significantly impact the convergence between pre-layout and post-layout timing. Thus, there is a definite need for preliminary (estimated) R/C and timing information from the back-end, to be available up-front during logic synthesis.

The second issue is that there is little or no information being exchanged between logic synthesis and placement and routing tools and hence there is no guarantee of convergence to a working design within a few iterations. The primary reason for both these limitations is the difference between the design database that contains the logical information and the design database that contains the physical information. The back-end tools operate largely on the latter while the front-end tools operate largely on the former. Since net delays are dependent on accurate estimations of the net capacitance and resistance, at smaller geometries, it is important to accurately predict R/Cs for a design in the initial stages (i.e., front-end logic synthesis phase). Also, required is a means to communicate changes in the netlist information during synthesis to back-end tools so that incremental placement and routing mechanism is supported. This feature in placement & route tools is called an Engineering Change Order (ECO). It helps maintain the results from the previous placement and route iteration and perform incremental changes like adding cells, removing cells and changing placement of specific cells in the design.

In general, placement and routing of a medium sized ASIC takes anywhere from one to two weeks to complete one iteration depending on the specifics of the flow used. This includes the time involved in netlist preparation for placement and routing, pad ring generation, ironing out name mismatch issues etc. Thus, a floor-planning tool, which can perform netlist placement and estimate the loads can significantly speed up the design flow. Further, the synthesis tool should have the capability to take the physical hierarchy information along with the estimated/extracted R/C values from the back-end tools and use this information during synthesis.

7.2 Floor-planning—Link Between Front-End and Back-End

To address the disconnect between the front-end and the back-end and allow flow of information between the two, a good floor-planning environment is critical—one that is tightly integrated with synthesis, placement and routing tools, static timing analysis tools, clock-tree synthesis and analysis tools which give various information reports. Floor-planning tools which work at the Register Transfer Level (RTL) to estimate parameters like area, timing, congestion, power etc. are in development and will soon be a part of the fundamental ASIC design flow in the future.

The OVI industry standard format Physical Design Exchange Format (PDEF) is used for exchanging physical hierarchy information between the floor-planning environment and synthesis. This allows synthesis to have visibility into the physical location of the cells on the die and hence calculate the net delays more accurately for each physical cluster. However, while PDEF has information about the clusters, cell location it does not have information about routing resources, congestion or die size.

Standard Delay Format (SDF) is another OVI standard which is used for communicating delay information between the floor-planning and synthesis environment. Estimated or extracted net capacitance and resistance information is communicated via Standard Parasitic Format (SPF) or via synthesis tool specific scripts. Also, after floor-planning a design specific wire-load model can be generated which can be used during synthesis for more accurate RC estimation for nets. There are provisions to generate wire-load models for each physical cluster. The floor-planning environment can interact with back-end placement and route tools using a netlist format such as Design Exchange Format (DEF) which is currently a format developed by Cadence Design Systems, Inc. Among other things DEF supports passing placement information in the netlist.

7.3 File Formats

In this section, we discuss certain basic file formats that enable the design flow (Table 1). In general, a timing driven approach is mandatory both at the front-end and back-end for designs targeted to process geometries less that 0.35 micron technology. The recommended flow is largely independent of EDA tools used. In other words, it is based on industry standard formats for exchange of information between tools. The starting point for this flow is a mapped netlist derived from synthesis using statistical wire-load models available in the library.

Table 1: File Formats

File	Expansion	Description
LEF* LLEF/PLEF	Library Export Format	Format developed by Cadence
DEF*	Design Export Format	Format developed by Cadence
DSPF	Detailed Standard Parasitic Format	Industry standard format. Similar to spice format
SDF	Standard Delay Format	Industry standard format giving pin to pin delays
PDEF	Physical Data Exchange Format	Industry Standard format for physical cluster and placement information (initiated by Synopsys)

* THE VSIA has succeeded in bringing LEF and DEF formats to the public domain.

LEF and DEF are both ASCII files. While LEF is description of the technology library cells, DEF is an ASCII description of the instances in the design and their connectivity. These formats are specific to the Cadence placement and route tools. Other EDA vendors for placement and route have their equivalent formats which are not discussed in this book. The intent here is to illustrate the flow rather than to promote one flow or format over another. Logical Library Exchange Format (LLEF) and Physical Library Exchange Format (PLEF) are commonly used formats which are extensions to the LEF.

7.3.1   SDF Timing File

Example 7.1   SDF File Back-annotated from Floor-planning

```
(DELAYFILE
(SDFVERSION "OVI 1.0")
 (DESIGN "top")
 (DATE "Mar-16-96")
 (DIVIDER.)
 (VOLTAGE)
 (PROCESS "")
  (TEMPERATURE )
  (TIMESCALE 1 ns)

  (CELL (CELLTYPE "an05d2")
   (INSTANCE U11)
   (DELAY (ABSOLUTE
    (IOPATH A4 Z (1.174:1.174:1.174) (.862:.862:.862))
    (IOPATH A2 Z (1.168:1.168:1.168) (.772:.772:.772))
    (IOPATH A5 Z (1.219:1.219:1.219) (.845:.845:.845))
    (IOPATH A3 Z (1.252:1.252:1.252) (.801:.801:.801))
    (IOPATH A1 Z (1.309:1.309:1.309) (.787:.787:.787))
   ))
  )
 . .
 . .
 . .


  (CELL (CELLTYPE "dfntnb")
   (INSTANCE I1.int_count_reg_3)
   (DELAY (ABSOLUTE
    (IOPATH CP Q (1.144:1.144:1.144) (.797:.797:.797))
    (IOPATH CP QN (.714:.714:.714) (.794:.794:.794))
   ))
   (TIMINGCHECK
    (SETUP D (posedge CP) (.280))
    (HOLD D (posedge CP) (.000))
    (WIDTH  (posedge CP) (.300))
    (WIDTH  (negedge CP) (.350))
```

```
   )
  )
..
..
..


  (CELL (CELLTYPE "top")
  (INSTANCE )
  (DELAY (ABSOLUTE
    (INTERCONNECT  U11.Z I2.int_count_reg_3.CP (.050:.050:.050)
(.052:.052:.052))
..
..
..

    (INTERCONNECT  I2.int_count_reg_0.Q U12.A1 (.006:.006:.006)
(.006:.006:.006))
    (INTERCONNECT  I2.int_count_reg_0.Q I2.U7.A2
(.007:.007:.007) (.007:.007:.007))
  ))
  )
)
```

In addition to the formats in Table 1, other information needed to make the flow possible includes SDF path constraints, output port loads, input port slew rates, clock skews and their period and waveforms. SDF Path constraints can be written out from synthesis tools to capture the required path delay constraints between sequential elements, between IOs as well as between IOs and sequential elements.

Example 7.1 shows an SDF file written out from a commercial floor-planning tool. The SDF file provides information about the estimated cell and net delay from floor-planning evaluations. There are two delays defined in the SDF file IOPATH and INTERCONNECT delay. The IOPATH delay is the cell intrinsic delay and the INTERCONNECT delay is the net connect delay. The Floor-planner tool may choose to lump the net transition (load) delay either with the IOPATH or the INTERCONNECT delay. Also, the setup and hold check information is provided for the sequential elements.

7.3.2   SDF Path Constraints

```
(CELL
  (CELLTYPE "COUNT_SEQ_VHDL")
   (INSTANCE)
   (TIMINGCHECK
      (PATHCONSTRAINT SEEN_TRAILING_reg/CP SEEN_TRAILING_reg/Q
U114/A U114/Z U93/A U93/Z U92/B U92/Z U95/A U95/Z U111/A U111/Z
U98/A U98/Z COUNT_reg\[1\]/D (3.200:3.200:3.200) )
  )
 )
 )
```

These SDF path constraints can be forward-annotated to back-end
tools. For example, the floorplanner and/or the placement and routing
tool on reading the SDF file in Example 7.2 interprets that the required
time for the path starting SEEN_TRAILING_reg/CP and ending at
COUNT_reg\[1\]/D is 3.2.

The output loads and the input port slew rates are required to accurately
calculate the delays using the estimated/extracted RC and the cell
delays from the technology timing library.

7.3.3   Physical Views and Technology Information

Physical views of the technology libraries as well as other technology
specific information such as metal layer information, preferred routing
directions of metal layers etc. are also required for the design flow. For
every cell, logical and timing information are required for the
floor-planning environment.

The LLEF and PLEF models of a 2-input AND gate are shown below.
The LLEF file contains information such as pin names and directions;
size, orientation, intrinsic delay numbers and other information.

Example 7.2   LLEF

```
macro and2a0
   class core ;
   foreign and2a0 -1.200000 -1.150000 ;
```

```
size 14.00 by 29.45 ;
symmetry x y ;
site compute 0.00 0.00 N do 1 by 1 step 55.00 55.90 ;
site compute 7.00 0.00 FN do 1 by 1 step 55.00 55.90 ;
pin Y
  foreign Y ;
  direction output ;
  use signal ;
  vhi 0.5 ;
  vlo 0.3 ;
  risevoltagethreshold 0.4 ;
  fallvoltagethreshold 0.4 ;
end Y
pin A
  foreign A ;
  direction input ;
  use signal ;
  capacitance 0.018 ;
  vhi 0.5 ;
  vlo 0.3 ;
  risevoltagethreshold 0.4 ;
  fallvoltagethreshold 0.4 ;
end A
pin B
  foreign B ;
  direction input ;
  use signal ;
  capacitance 0.020 ;
  vhi 0.5 ;
  vlo 0.3 ;
  risevoltagethreshold 0.4 ;
  fallvoltagethreshold 0.4 ;
end B
pin VDD
  foreign VDDA: ;
  direction input ;
  use power ;
  shape feedthru ;
end VDD
```

```
  pin GND
     foreign GNDA: ;
     direction input ;
     use ground ;
     shape feedthru ;
   end GND
   timing
     frompin A ; topin Y ;
     fall intrinsic 0.145 0.324 0.050 0.171 0.372 0.150 0.186
0.421 0.300 variable 1.000 1.814 ;
     rise intrinsic 0.188 0.387 0.050 0.268 0.487 0.150 0.357
0.605 0.300 variable 1.114 2.339 ;
     unateness noninvert ;
     frompin B ; topin Y ;
     fall intrinsic 0.172 0.379 0.050 0.213 0.438 0.150 0.261
0.511 0.300 variable 1.007 1.832 ;
     rise intrinsic 0.179 0.395 0.050 0.235 0.458 0.150 0.286
0.538 0.300 variable 1.129 2.346 ;
     unateness noninvert ;
   end timing
end and2a0
```

Example 7.3   PLEF Example

```
MACRO and2a0
  PIN A
  PORT
    LAYER poly ;
       RECT 5.10 7.75 6.50 9.15 ;
  END
  PORT
    LAYER poly ;
       RECT 5.10 14.75 6.50 16.15 ;
  END
  PORT
    LAYER poly ;
       RECT 5.10 17.25 6.50 18.65 ;
  END
  END A
  PIN B
```

```
PORT
  LAYER poly ;
    RECT 0.50 7.75 1.90 9.15 ;
  END
  END B
. . .
. . .
. . .
  OBS
    LAYER m1 ; /* size of obstruction on metal layer 1 */
    RECT 5.10 12.45 6.50 18.65 ;
    RECT 4.20 17.25 5.10 18.65 ;
    RECT 6.50 17.25 8.90 18.65 ;
    RECT 2.80 17.25 4.20 25.65 ;
  VIA 3.5 24.95 via01 ; /* via from layer 0 to layer 1 */
  VIA 3.5 22.65 via01 ;
  VIA 5.8 13.15 via01 ;
  VIA 8.2 17.95 via01 ;
  VIA 3.5 20.25 via01 ;
  END
END and2a0
```

Example 7.4 shows a technology file which contains information about the fabrication technology such as metal layers, routing direction on a metal layer, wire widths, via, poly information etc.

Example 7.4   Technology Information

```
(technology test
  (layer m1 /* Metal layer m1 is horizontal with a 2300 micon
pitch and 1500 micron width */
    (spacing 800)
    (sameNetSpacing 800 stack)
    (wirewidths
      (width default 2500)
    )
    (pitch 2300)
    (direction horizontal)
    (cPerMicron 0.2)
```

```
    (cPerSq 0.0643)
    (rPerSq 0.074)
  )
  (layer m2
    (direction vertical)
    (spacing 800)
    (sameNetSpacing 700)
    (wirewidths
      (width default 1300)
    )
    (pitch 2300)
    (cPerMicron 0.17)
    (cPerSq 0.0313)
    (rPerSq 0.037)
  )
  (layer m3
    (direction horizontal)
    (spacing 700)
    (sameNetSpacing 700)
    (wirewidths
      (width default 1400)
    )
    (pitch 2300)
    (cPerMicron 0.2)
    (cPerSq 0.0246)
    (rPerSq 0.037)
  )
  (via via01
    (type default)
    (gdsiiAlias XX_MPOLY)
    (top poly (size 1500 1400))
    (comment under size cut01 for viewing purpose)
    (middle cut01 (size 500 500))
    (bottom m1 (size 1500 1400))
  )
  (sameNetRule cut01 cut01 700)
  (sameNetRule cut12 cut12 700)
  (sameNetRule cut23 cut23 700)
  (sameNetRule cut01 cut12 700 stack)
```

```
(sameNetRule cut12 cut23 700)
(sameNetRule cut01 cut23 0 stack)
)
```

7.3.4   Physical Delay Exchange Format (PDEF)

PDEF is the industry standard format initiated by Synopsys for exchanging physical cluster information between DC and back-end tools. The PDEF file contains physical cluster information generated from floor-planning or from the Design Compiler. It is possible to group cells in DC using the group command with the -soft option. This is used when the user wishes to group a certain list of cells into a specific group during placement. This is usually done for timing critical cells such as datapath logic cells. If they are not grouped together, it is possible that the floor-planning tool might spread the placement of these cells across the layout instead of placing them close together. This information can be forward-annotated to the floor-planner by writing out PDEF from DC using the Synopsys Floorplan Manager.

Example 7.5   PDEF File

```
(CLUSTERFILE
    (PDEFVERSION "1.0")
    (DESIGN "top")
    (DATE "Sat Mar 16 11:33:10 1996")
    (VENDOR "COMPASS")
    (PROGRAM "ChipPlanner-GA")
    (VERSION "v8r4.9.0")
    (DIVIDER /)
    (CLUSTER (NAME "I2")
        (UTILIZATION .4328)
        (MAX_UTILIZATION 100.0000)
        (CELL (NAME I2/int_count_reg_2))
        (CELL (NAME I2/int_count_reg_3))
        (CELL (NAME I2/U8))
        (CELL (NAME I2/U11))
        (CELL (NAME I2/U10))
        (CELL (NAME I2/U7))
        (CELL (NAME I2/int_count_reg_1))
```

```
            (CELL (NAME I2/int_count_reg_0))
            (CELL (NAME I2/U9))
      )
      (CLUSTER (NAME "top_ga")
            (UTILIZATION .4379)
            (MAX_UTILIZATION 100.0000)
            (CELL (NAME U11))
            (CELL (NAME TC_reg))
            (CELL (NAME U12))
      )
      (CLUSTER (NAME "I1")
            (UTILIZATION .4361)
            (MAX_UTILIZATION 100.0000)
            (CELL (NAME I1/int_count_reg_1))
            (CELL (NAME I1/int_count_reg_0))
            (CELL (NAME I1/U9))
            (CELL (NAME I1/U7))
            (CELL (NAME I1/U8))
            (CELL (NAME I1/U10))
            (CELL (NAME I1/int_count_reg_2))
            (CELL (NAME I1/int_count_reg_3))
            (CELL (NAME I1/U11))
      )
)
```

Example 7.5 shows a PDEF file written out by a commercial Floor-planner. The PDEF file shows three clusters for this design: I1, I2 and top_ga. Also, information provided in the PDEF file is the actual cell instance names in each of the clusters.

7.4 Floor-Planning Concepts

The netlist and the SDF path constraints generated from logic synthesis form the inputs to any floor-planning tool. Floor-planning techniques and methodologies differ depending on whether the target is a standard cell or gate array technology. In gate arrays only the metal interconnection layers can be customized while the sea of gates architecture is fixed for every ASIC. For standard cells, on the other hand, all the fabrication layers can be customized.

A design netlist can be divided into the following: core cells, IO cells and macros (RAMs, ROMs etc.). In general, IOs are pre-placed by the user since they are often determined by the system requirements. The macros such as RAMs, ROMs and embedded Intellectual Property (IP) etc. can be automatically placed by the block placer. In general, they should be manually placed by the designer with the intent of minimizing congestion in routing. The core cells are automatically placed by the timing driven placement tool using the *grouping and regioning* information provided by the designer.

For gate arrays, the base die is fixed and pre-designed using a base die generation software. It specifies the size of the core, and the number of rows and columns of the sea of gates architecture. To incorporate embedded blocks, a regions of the base die are cut out and demarcated for a required size. For standard cells based on the number of core cells and macros in the design, a base die of an estimated P&R boundary is created in the floor-planning environment. This is followed by placing the IO pads around the core placement and routing region. One way to pre-place IOs could be through DEF, which supports pre-placement of cells.

7.4.1 Grouping and Regioning

There are two concepts very commonly used in floor-planning and placement, namely, *Grouping and Regioning*. The function of a group is to define a set of components that should be placed close together. The designer based on his knowledge of the design can guide the tool in the placement of logical hierarchy blocks. A typical example is datapath logic in a design, where the designer has a definite understanding of a required specific order of instances for placement purposes. Regioning is the process of defining an area of the die within which a set of components or blocks can be placed. Grouping and regioning help localize the problem for placement to local clusters. However, excessive grouping and/or regioning can restrict the placer from generating optimal results.

After IO pad assignment, the next step is to create logical groups for the different core cells in the design. Grouping based on logical hierarchy is the most common approach since it allows some co-relation between the synthesis phase and the physical phase. The main advantage of creating groups is that it narrows down the problem space. Note that we have not assigned any location to the groups on the die. Based on the groups we created in the previous step, we should then analyze it for routing congestion, density of cells in a group etc. The feedback from the analysis can be used to tweak the grouping of cells. In general it is recommended to merge logical hierarchies together if it helps timing and routing but avoid splitting logical hierarchies to different locations on the die. This is because the custom wire-load models created later in the flow for physical groups or clusters cannot be used during synthesis if one logical hierarchy has two different wire-load models associated with it. One criteria used as a feedback from analysis is the ratio of number of cells in a group and the number of external nets fanning-in/out of the block. Also, since we have not pre-placed any macros yet, this analysis should give you a feel on whether they should be merged with any group or not.

Once you have created the different groups, then comes the task of assigning them to regions or locations on the die. This can be done automatically through knowledge of the design and by providing guidance to the block placement tool can considerably improve the quality of results. The block placer algorithm could use a minimum connectivity based algorithm which could optimize the routing congestion and indirectly improve timing. Alternately, the block placer algorithm used could be timing driven where the placer is driven by the SDF path constraints to decide placement based on timing constraints. In general, macros should either be placed manually or through automatic placement. They can then be moved based on feedback from analysis. For the timing-driven approach a very tight integration with the cell delay calculator (DC) is required.

7.4.2   Manual Placement of Hard Macros

The placement of macros can have a significant impact on the flexibility that is available to the place and route tool. Hence, it is important that certain basic rules are adhered to when manually placing macros in the layout. For instance, it is advisable not to place macros in the centre of the die as in figure 7.2. A large macro in the middle of a layout could mean a lot of routes having to by-pass the macro. This could cause congestion.

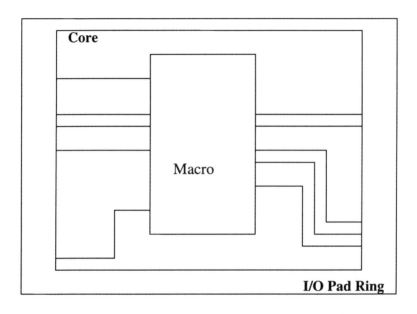

Figure 7.2 Macro at the center of the layout (bad placement)

At the same time, location of the macros depends on the interface from the macro to the rest of the design as well as the chip interface. In general, it is desirable to place macros towards the periphery of the layout where there are IOs connected to it and allow continuous room for the standard cells, rather than have to by-pass the macros as shown in Figure 7.3. Then, in order to prevent the placement tool from placing cells very close around the macro, create "cannotoccupy" regions around the macro to reserve space for routing. The amount of room is usually dependent on the technology and the power consumption of the macro. Also, it is important to adjust the orientation of the placement of the macro in such a way as to avoid having pins on the side where there are less routing tracks available.

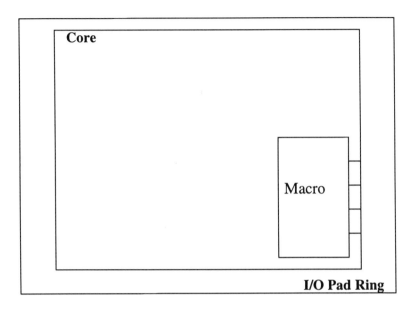

Figure 7.3 Macro at periphery with connectivity to the I/O pad ring

After the placement/regioning of all the soft logic groups and macros the next step is to run global routing analysis on the chip to get feedback on global channel congestion, placement of soft logic groups and macros. Also, optimization on the placement of the pins on the soft groups can be done to reduce congestion. If the global routing analysis gives good results, then the block and macro placement at the top level can be frozen and the task of floor-planning, placing and routing the individual soft blocks can be handled independently and in parallel. A good floorplan is one in which there are minimum intra-cluster nets at the top level.

The above discussion is by and large restricted to standard cell placement and routing tools. For gate arrays, the die size and the number of rows and columns is fixed. The floor-plan i.e. dedicated routing area and dedicated placement area of the gate array is pre-defined. Hence, if the global routing analysis shows heavy routing congestion even after trying different block placement, then, it might be required to manually increase the die size etc. and start all over again.

For standard cells you can either have a variable die or a fixed die approach. The variable die approach is a channel-router based algorithm which can add more routing tracks if required based on feedback from the global routing congestion analysis. The variable die approach is common for 2-layer metal technology. In the fixed area approach (common for 3 layer metal technology) the number of routing tracks cannot increase but the size of the rows and columns can be increased dynamically based on feedback from congestion analysis.

7.4.3   Placement of Core Cells

After the placement of macros, the next step is to run the placement tool to place the core primitive cells. In general, placement tools are specifically targeted for Gate Arrays or for standard cells (e.g., Gate Ensemble from Cadence for Gate Arrays and Cell3/Silicon Ensemble for standard cells). Most floor-planning tools have an in-built placer that performs placement and generates quick analysis results. It is important that this placement tool be the same as the placement tool used during actual placement and route in order to get consistent results (estimated capacitance and resistance) after floor-planning and after placement and routing. This issue arises when tools from different EDA vendors are used for floor-planning and placement and routing. During placement of standard cells it is important to leave room for power/ground routing channels (for example, about 25 micron width for 0.35 micron standard cells).

Having completed the floorplan for all levels of hierarchy the next step is to generate the following information for feedback to the logical domain (i.e., the synthesis environment):

1. A custom wire-load model specific to the design (load file to generate custom wire load models from the synthesis tool).
2. Estimated RC
3. SDF file with estimated delays
4. Physical hierarchy information in PDEF format.

7.4.4   Post-placement Steps

After placement of the core cells, a custom wire-load model is generated for each hierarchical block in the design using the average capacitance and resistance values of the nets in different fanout groups. This custom wire-load model can then be used during synthesis to optimize the design with more accurate wire-load models.

The R/Cs and SDF have estimated values because at this stage the actual routing has not been completed. After completion of actual routing the values will no longer be estimated but true accurate extracted values. For estimation, the routing between pins is estimated using algorithms like the Steiner tree algorithm or a minimum spanning tree algorithm. In general, the accuracy of estimated values should be within 5-10% of extracted values in order to guarantee convergence after final routing.

Ideally, an accurate delay calculator engine should be embedded in the floor-planning environment to calculate net delays from the estimated Arcs and cell delay information from the libraries to generate a SDF timing file. Alternately, the output from extraction must be provided to a delay calculator to generate timing information. For DSM technologies it is critical that non-linear lookup table models be supported to model the non-linear effects of the DSM technology.

7.5   Parasitic Extraction

Accurate extraction of the resistance and capacitance on a placed and routed design database is critical, particularly in DSM designs where interconnect delays account for over 50% of the delay. But as design sizes increase rapidly, the process of extraction has become extremely time consuming. There are several algorithmic approaches to extraction including "true 3D", "quasi-3D" and "2-D". In this section we describe parasitic extraction in general—the extraction flow, the distinction between extraction and estimation. The different file formats involved have been discussed in section 7.4.

There are different stages of the design flow at which extraction can be performed. Firstly, extraction can be performed on the fully routed design database or on the routed LEF/DEF database (i.e., at the abstract level) in a Cadence place and route flow. Secondly, extraction can be performed on the full-chip gdsII after the completion of the Layout vs. Schematic (LVS) process. Generating full-chip gdsII database usually happens at the final stage of the design flow. The abstract level database on the other hand is available prior to the LVS process.

7.5.1   Extraction vs. Estimation

Parasitic Estimation is performed after floor-planning and placement (not routing) of the design. Estimation is performed at abstract level—LEF and placed DEF level when using Cadence tools for placement and routing. However, the values generated from this estimation approach are less accurate than those generated after routing since they do not take into consideration the actual routing of the design but instead use "estimates".

The estimated parasitics are used to generate custom wire load models as discussed in chapter 1. The accuracy of the estimates is critical since these custom wire-load models drive the logic synthesis process. The idea is to provide efficient estimates early in the design cycle and thereby guide the synthesis tool to generate a design that meets timing after complete routing. Hence, it is important that the "estimation" algorithm used after floor-planning and placement and the "extraction" algorithm used after layout do not differ significantly.

Parasitic Extraction on the other hand is performed on a placed and routed design. There are two possible approaches to extraction—one at the LEF/DEF level (when using Cadence tools for placement and routing) and the other after Layout vs. Schematic (LVS) verification. While the former involves extraction at an "abstact" level, the latter involves extraction at the layout level. The former provides a means to extract the loads early in the design cycle without having to wait until completion of the LVS process on the design. However, the post-LVS extraction is more accurate but involves longer run times than the LEF/DEF level extraction.

LVS is the final verification step in the design process and involves comparing the full-chip layout database (gdsII) with the netlist generated from logic synthesis. Extraction at the LVS level is usually at the very end of the design cycle just prior to tape out. Both forms of extraction are based on a "rule" file generated from process specific data.

7.5.2   Extraction Techniques

Parasitic extraction techniques can be divided into four main categories, namely, lumped C, full-chip R/C, selective R/C and smart R/C.

Lumped C: In this approach, the net capacitance (C) is calculated while resistance (R) is ignored. This technique is the fastest among all the available techniques in terms of the run-time. However, it is less accurate since it does not model resistance. As designs move to smaller process technologies a lumped C approach is unlikely identify all the timing issues. In other words, the impact of resistance must be considered.

Full chip R/C: This the most time consuming approach because RC extraction is performed on every node in the design. Since run-times are extremely long a full chip RC can sometimes be an "overkill". This approach is certainly the preferred approach provided run-times can be improved.

Selective R/C: This approach is a combination of lumped C and extraction of R on a selected group of nets. The intent here is to identify a set of potential problem nets and perform R/C extraction only on those while lumped C on the rest of the cells. In this case, the user provides the list of nets for which R/C is to be extracted. (e.g., clock nets)

Smart R/C: This approach is considered to be a "smart" approach because resistance (R) is calculated only for those nets that cross a certain capacitance threshold. A lumped capacitance (C) extraction is performed on all the remaining nets.

Listed below are some issues that one must be aware of when performing parasitic extraction. The data generated from parasitic extraction is fed back into the static timing and synthesis environments.

- In the deep sub-micron technologies (0.35 micron and below) it is advisable not to ignore resistance.

- Distributed RC extraction, which takes resistive nature of nets into account is the most accurate, but a very compute intensive process. A good trade-off between time and accuracy is to do a full RC extraction for critical nets and a C-only extraction on all other nets. Critical nets are those for which the effective capacitance is above a certain threshold value which can be controlled by the user.

- The pin capacitance for cells is typically in the library file. The extraction tool should make sure that it does not duplicate the capacitance for any layout area (poly, metal, vias etc.) that has already been included in the pin capacitance.

- The values of extracted net capacitances ultimately depend on accurate process characterization. The rule files used for extraction should be built with accurate representation of the process technology.

- In a hierarchical placement and route flow, it is likely that extraction is performed on individual sub-modules. However, it is important that full-chip extraction is performed to get accurate net capacitances due to inter-block connections.

7.6 Clock-Tree Synthesis

After logic synthesis, the design is taken to the Floor-planner and the Place and Route tool to create clock-trees on all clock sources (clock nets) in the design. In order to build the clock tree the following information must be provided:

1. Levels of buffers desired for the clock tree.

2. The kinds of buffers (BUFA or BUFB or BUFC) desired at each level. (where BUFA, BUFB and BUFC are buffer cells from the technology library)

3. At each level, should the buffer outputs to be shorted.

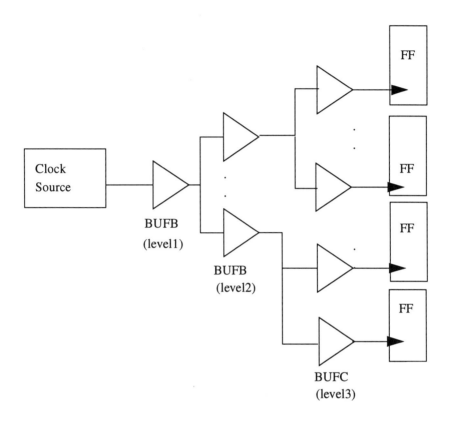

Figure 7.4 Clock Tree example

A static timing analysis tool like DesignTime can be used to determine the number of sequential elements driven by a certain clock source. For example, Synopsys DesignTime has the command:

```
report_transitive_fanout -clock_tree
```

This command when executed gives the list of flip-flops in the fanout network of each clock source. Clock sources which feed large number of flip-flops would need more number of levels in the clock tree. After generating the clock-tree it is possible to generate a report on the clock skews. Figure 7.4 shows an example of a clock tree with multiple levels of buffers.

To minimize clock skews it is desirable to use large buffer sizes at each level. Also, the number of levels must be selected in such a manner that each level does not have a large fanout (less than 20, as a rule of thumb). You may choose to short the buffer outputs only if it helps balance the skews better.

The clock tree synthesis tool tries to place buffers with the intent of balancing skews, but it is not guaranteed that small skews will be achieved for a given clock source. Further, balancing skews between different clock tree networks originating from different clock sources can be a tricky issue for clock synthesis tools. Hence, it is likely to involve some "hand crafting".

7.7 Synopsys Floorplan Manager

The *Floorplan Manager* from Synopsys helps ensure an effective link between Design Compiler and floor-planning and place and route tools. Figure 7.5 shows the iterative loop between the Synopsys Design Compiler and the Floorplan Manager. The intent is to capture estimated load, resistance and delay information after placement (but no routing) and use this information during synthesis. This helps restrict the number of iterations that might be required between the front-end and the back-end after actual routing has been performed. Interchange of information between these tools is accomplished using Standard Delay Format (SDF), Physical Data Exchange Format (PDEF), and Resistance/Load script.

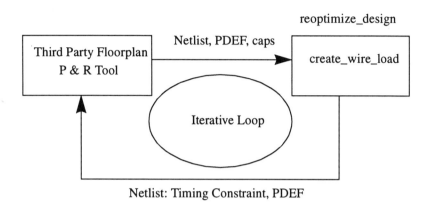

Figure 7.5 Iterative loop between Floor-planning and Synthesis

The following steps describe the links to layout flow using the Synopsys Floorplan Manager.

1. Synthesize the design to gates using the statistical wire-load models provided in the technology library. This is likely to be inaccurate since wire-loads are very much design and layout dependent. At this stage, one can write out timing constraint information in SDF from DC for timing driven floor-planning/place & route tools.

2. Perform floorplaning, followed by placement of the entire design. Pre-placement, grouping and regions are performed at this stage. Generate the cluster information (PDEF), estimated parasitics (RC) and delay values (SDF).

3. Back-annotate physical information from placement to the Floorplan Manager. Create custom wire-load models for your design based on the back-annotated data. This wire-load can be based on "physical" grouping performed during step two.

4. Perform static timing analysis on the design after back-annotation. If the timing violations are relatively large, re-synthesize design beginning with source HDL and new wire-load models generated in step 3. On the other hand if the timing violations are small, reoptimize

the design using the `reoptimize_design` command with the `-post_layout` option. This option allows greater flexibility in making changes to the design since at this stage actual routing has not been performed. Generate the netlist after re-synthesis, new PDEF and SDF file for further floor-planning.

5. Repeat steps 2, 3 and 4 until the design meets timing with positive slack. Then proceed to perform complete routing and generate back-annotation data in SDF, PDEF and parasitics (`set_load`/`set_resistance`)

6. At this point, the timing violations, if any, should be fixed by performing in place optimization on the design using the `reoptimize_design -ipo` command.

7.7.1 Generating Custom Wire-Load Models

Wire load models are extremely design dependent. Hence, it is required to generate design specific wire load models for synthesis to ensure near optimal results prior to placement and route. Synopsys Design Compiler provides a mechanism to generate custom wire load models based on back annotated load information.

Example 7.6 shows a custom wire-load model generated from a commercial floor-planning tool. This custom wire load model can be included in your technology library using the update_lib command and then selected appropriately using the set_wire_load_model command. Alternately, one can manually add the wire load model to the technology library source file (.lib file). These estimated wire-loads are not as accurate as actual wire-loads based on place and route generated wire loads. However, these wire-loads do minimize the number of elaborate, time consuming place and route cycles that one has to go through before arriving at an accurate wire model.

The following are the steps for generating custom wire load models using the Synopsys Design Compiler:

1. Perform placement of design netlist using a placement/floor-planning tool.

2. Generate estimated load file (`set_load` file). Most commercial placement tools generate this information.

3. Read netlist into Design Compiler

4. Include `set_load` script.

5. Use the `create_wire_load` command (use `-hierarchy` option to generate custom wire load for all sub-designs. Check Design Compiler reference manual for `create_wire_load` command options).

Example 7.6   Custom Wire-load Model

```
/*  Synopsys wire load models for design top */
/*  format: fanout_length(fanout, length, average_cap, std_dev,
points); */
wire_load("compass_wl") {
 resistance : 0;
 capacitance : 1;
 area : 0;
 slope : 0.48;
 fanout_length(  1,   0.26,   0.26,   0.059,   11);
 fanout_length(  2,   0.26,   0.26,   0.16,   2);
 fanout_length(  3,   0.62,   0.62,   0.066,   6);
 fanout_length(  4,   1.1,   1.1,   0.2,   1);
}
```

7.8 Methodology Audit

1. Does the current methodology being followed involve the transfer of SDF constraint files from the synthesis environment to the place and route tools? In other words, do you follow a timing driven placement and route approach?

2. Is initial placement (and no routing) and custom wire-load model generation a part of the current design flow? Are these wire load models used to re-optimize the design?

3. Are you currently using commercial floor-planning tools or is floor-planning a "back of the napkin" effort?

4. How many iterations do you typically go through between the front end and back-end. Ideally, there should not be more than three iterations—one for placement and estimated loads, the second for actual routing after re-synthesizing using custom wire load models, and the third after in-place optimization.

5. Is post-layout static timing analysis a part of the current design flow?

6. Are you currently using one delay calculator across the design flow. Most tools perform some form of delay calculation and very often these delay calculators need not produce identical results.

7. Is in-place optimization part of the current design flow? Is the technology library equipped with footprints in order to perform in-place optimization.

8. If you design your own I/Os do you have a set of Electro-Static Discharge (ESD) requirements for them ?

9. What techniques are currently being used for clock skew estimation? Have these techniques been correlated against a "golden" simulation using Hspice?

10. Have the memories in the design been placed at the periphery of the layout?

Appendix A

A.1 EDA Tools and Vendors

This section lists several EDA vendor tools for simulation, synthesis, power, static timing analysis, placement and routing, parasitic extraction and formal verification. This is far from an exhaustive list. With acquisitions and other changes in the EDA industry its unlikely that this list will remain current. However, the intent is to give the reader a quick look at few of the available commercial tools.

Table 1: Logic Simulation

Simulator	EDA Vendor
Verilog-XL (Verilog).	Cadence Design Systems
Leapfrog (VHDL)	Cadence Design Systems
VCS (Verilog)	Chronologic (Synopsys)
V-System (VHDL/Verilog)	Model Technology.
TimeMill(Transistor level)	Epic (Synopsys)
VSS (VHDL)	Synopsys

Table 2: Hardware Accelerators/Interfaces

Simulator	EDA Vendor
Voyager CSX (VHDL)	IKOS

Table 2: Hardware Accelerators/Interfaces

Simulator	EDA Vendor
Gemini CSX (Verilog)	IKOS

Table 3: Cycle-Based Simulators

Simulator	EDA Vendor
SpeedSim (VHDL)	Quickturn
PureSpeed (Verilog)	Frontline Design Automation (Avant!)
Vantage UltraSpec (VHDL)	Viewlogic (Synopsys)
FinSim ECST	Fintronic USA
Cobra	Cadence Design Systems
Cyclone	Synopsys

Table 4: Formal Verification

Tool	EDA Vendor
Formality	Synopsys
DesignVerifyer	Chrysalis
CheckOff/Lambda	Abstract, Inc.
VFormal	Compass Design Automation (Avant!)
FormalCheck	Bell Labs Design Automation

Table 5: Static Timing Analysis

Tool	EDA Vendor
PrimeTime	Synopsys
DesignTime	Synopsys
Motive	Viewlogic (Synopsys)
Velocity	Mentor Graphics
PathMill	Epic (Synopsys)
Pearl	Cadence Design Systems

Table 6: Parasitic Extraction

Tool	EDA Vendors
Arcadia	Epic (Synopsys)
Star-Extract	Avant!
Fire&Ice	Simplex Solutions
HyperExtract	Cadence Design Systems

Table 7: Logic Synthesis

Tool	EDA Vendors
Design Compiler	Synopsys
BuildGates	Ambit Design Systems
Galileo (FPGA)	Examplar (Mentor Graphics)
FPGA Express (FPGA)	Synopsys
Synplify (FPGA)	Synplicity

Table 8: Power

Tool	EDA Vendor
DesignPower	Synopsys
Power Compiler	Synopsys
Power Mill	Epic (Synopsys)
CoolIt!	InterHDL
Watt Watcher	Sente

Table 9: Placement & Routing

Tool	EDA Vendor
Silicon Ensemble, Gate Ensemble, IC Craftsman	Cadence
Apollo	Avant!
Grandmaster	Gambit
Gards, SonIC	Silicon Valley Research

Table 10: Emulation

Tool	EDA Vendor
CoBALT	Quickturn Systems
System Explorer	Aptix
SimExpress	Mentor
Avatar, VirtuaLogic	IKOS

Recommended Further Readings

1. Algorithms for VLSI Physical Design Automation, Naveed Sherwani. Kluwer Academic Publishers.

2. Logic Synthesis Using Synopsys, Second Edition Pran Kurup, Taher Abbasi, Kluwer Academic Publishers.

3. ASIC Design Flow Leads to First Silicon Success. Shekhar Patkar, Pran Kurup, Integrated System Design, August 97.

4. FSM Synthesis, Pran Kurup & Pradeep Fernandes. ASIC & EDA, Septemeber 1994.

5. Design VERIFYer Manual, Chrysalys Symbolic Design Inc.

6. Design Time Manual, Synopsys Inc.

7. Motive Reference Manual, Viewlogic. Inc.

8. Focus Report: HDL Simulation Tools, Steven E. Schulz

9. Focus Report: Timing Analysis Tools and Trends, Steven E. Schulz

10. Design Automation of a Receiver: Breaking the RTL cycle time barrier using BC. David Johnson, Motorola, DesignCon 98.

11. Behavioral Synthesis Speeds Designs, Reduces Complexity, Taher Abbasi, Pran Kurup. EDN-Asia, May 1996.

12. Designing a 100K gate set-top box ASIC using BC, SNUG 95. David Black.

13. The Verilog Hardware Description Language, Third Edition, Donald E. Thomas, Philip R. Moorby.

14. VHDL: Hardware Description and Design, Roger Lipsett, Carl Schaefer, Cary Ussery.

15. Digital Logic Simulation: Event-driven, Cycle-based, and Home-brewed. Clive Maxfield, EDN July 4, 1996.

16. Time Flies when you are analyzing it, Clive Maxfield, EDN August 1, 1996.

17. Low Power ASIC Design, Jerry Fenkil, ISD March 1997.

18. Unified ASIC Library Development Suite, Ricky Bedi, SIG-VHDL IFIP WG 10.5/ECSI TEMIC/MATRA MHS, April 1995, pp 126

19. Chip place-and-route tools lay it on the line, Jim Lipman, EDN March 26, 1998

20. Physical Design: Reminiscing and Looking Ahead., E.S. Kuh, Proc. of Int. Symp. on Physical Design, pp. 206, 1997.

21. Chip Hierarchical Design Systems (CHDS): A Foundation for Timing-Driven Physical Design into the 21st Century. R. G. Bushroe et al., Proc. of Int. Symp. on Physical Design, pp. 212-217, 1997.

22. The Quarter Micro Challenge: Integrating Physical and Logic Design R. Composano. Proc. of Int. Symp. on Physical Design, pp. 211, 1997.

23. The Future of Logic Synthesis and Physical Design in Deep Submicron Process Gemetries., K. Keutzer, A.R. Newton, N. Shenoy. Proc. of Int. Symp. on Physical Design, pp. 218-223, 1997.

24. Performance-Driven Soft-Macro Clustering and Placement by Preserving HDL Design Hierarchy., Hsiao-Pin Su, Allen C.-H. Wuand Youn-Long Lin, Proc. of Int. Symp. on Physical Designpp. 12-17, 1998.

25. Eight deadly sins in scan-based designs, Dr. Samy Makar, Dr. L.T. Wang, Bensen Cheung, Electronics Engineer, April 1998

26. At the Heart of Mixed-Signal SOC Design: Multiple Simulators, Andre Walker, Kevein Jorgensen, ISD Magazine May 1998

27. HDL Verification Coverage, Dean Darko, Paul B. Cohen, ISD Magazine, June 1998.

28. High-Performance Functional Validation, Mehdi Mohtashemi, Systems Science, Inc.

29. Spec-Based Verification, A New Methodology for Functional Verification of Systems/ASICs—A White Paper, http://www.verisity.com/

30. Assertion Synthesis, 0-In Design Automation. http://www.0-in.com/

31. The Ten Commandments of Excellent Design, Peter Chambers, Electronic Design, April 1997.